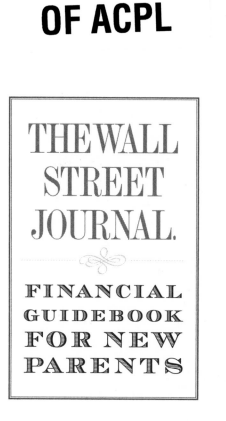

THE WALL
STREET
JOURNAL.

FINANCIAL
GUIDEBOOK
FOR NEW
PARENTS

THE WALL STREET JOURNAL.

FINANCIAL GUIDEBOOK FOR NEW PARENTS

STACEY L. BRADFORD

THREE RIVERS PRESS

NEW YORK

Published in the United States by Three Rivers Press, an imprint of
the Crown Publishing Group, a division of Random House, Inc., New York.
www.crownpublishing.com

Three Rivers Press and the Tugboat design are
registered trademarks of Random House, Inc.

Library of Congress Cataloging-in-Publication Data

Bradford, Stacey L.
The Wall Street Journal : financial guidebook for new parents /
Stacey L. Bradford.—1st ed.
  p. cm
Includes index.
1. Parents—United States—Finance, Personal.   2. Finance,
Personal—United States.   I. Title.
HG179.B67 2009
332.0240085'0973—dc22   2008050657

ISBN 978-0-307-40707-8

Printed in the United States of America

Design by Mauna Eichner and Lee Fukui

Illustrations: p. 19, © 2009 Alison Seiffer c/o theispot.com; p. 25, © 2009
Marc Rosenthal c/o theispot.com; p. 35, © 2009 Adam McCauley Collection
c/o theispot.com; p. 47, © 2009 Joyce Hesselberth c/o theispot.com; p. 65,
© 2009 William Rieser c/o theispot.com; p. 84, © 2009 Coco Masuda c/o
theispot.com; p. 98, © 2009 Chris Gash c/o theispot.com; p. 114, © 2009
Robert Saunders c/o theispot.com; p. 135, © 2009 Gordon Studer c/o
theispot.com; p. 156, © 2009 Riccardo Stampatori c/o theispot.com; p. 165,
© 2009 Dan Page c/o theispot.com; p. 175, © 2009 Travis Foster c/o
theispot.com

10 9 8 7 6 5 4 3 2 1

First Edition

TO RICK AND LEYNA

CONTENTS

INTRODUCTION:
NOW THE FUN BEGINS

1

PART ONE

WHEN BABY MAKES THREE

CHAPTER 1
YOUR MATERNITY
(OR PATERNITY) LEAVE

9

CHAPTER 2
KISSING THAT
CUBICLE GOOD-BYE

20

CHAPTER 3
RETURNING TO
THE GRIND

33

CHAPTER 4
WHO SAYS UNCLE SAM
DOESN'T CARE?

43

CHAPTER 5

WHERE SHOULD YOU NEST?

55

PART TWO

NO ONE EVER SAID KIDS WERE CHEAP

CHAPTER 6

FINDING (AND PAYING FOR) MARY POPPINS

75

CHAPTER 7

AVOIDING A HEALTH SCARE

93

CHAPTER 8

PAYING FOR HARVARD

107

PART THREE

YOUR CONTINGENCY PLAN

CHAPTER 9

YES, YOU NEED A WILL

125

CHAPTER 10

TRUSTS: THEY AREN'T JUST FOR THE WEALTHY

138

CHAPTER 11

LIFE INSURANCE:
BETTER SAFE THAN SORRY

148

CHAPTER 12

ACCIDENTS HAPPEN . . .
ARE YOU PREPARED?

161

MONEY-SAVING TIPS
FOR EVERY STAGE

170

Appendix

183

Acknowledgments

187

Index

189

INTRODUCTION
NOW THE FUN BEGINS

No one ever said having children was easy. First there are the 4:00 a.m. feedings, then the terrible twos, and before you know it, it's time to start worrying about those dreaded teenage years. *And* on top of the stress of caring for a child, you have to figure out how to cover all the expenses for one.

Ready for sticker shock? The average family spends between $11,000 and $16,000 raising their child during his first year and more than $200,000 before that child turns eighteen, according to the U.S. Department of Agriculture. Indulge in pricey items, such as a $900 Bugaboo stroller and private schools, and expenses can easily skyrocket to over $1 million. Add a second child and you had better expect to spend twice as much. (Sorry, folks, few economies of scale to be found here.) If parents don't have a handle on everything from child tax credits and the Family and Medical Leave Act of 1993 to flexible spending accounts and 529 plans, they could end up squandering precious dollars that will leave them coming up short just when it's time to pay for college.

Fortunately, there is a solution: planning. Trust me, I know it isn't easy to keep the big picture in mind when you have small children. Immediate expenses—such as outfitting a nursery—always seem to trump efforts to fund longer-term goals. After my daughter was born, I, too, found the experience bewildering and intimidating, and I write about this stuff for a living. It's one thing to know I should open a college fund and another to find the time to set one up in between feedings.

But—and this is good news!—the reality is that it didn't take nearly as much effort or time as I'd feared to set up a long-term plan for my new family. My husband and I attacked the project in three steps. First, we put our estate in order, then we set a budget for our immediate needs; finally, we tackled the proverbial elephant in the room—the college savings account. The challenge, of course, was how to balance all of this while continuing to fund our retirement.

We quickly realized that the only way to make our financial plan work was by keeping our baby-related spending to a minimum. Unfortunately, it proved much more difficult than we imagined not to get caught up in the race to keep up with the other moms and dads. While I was parking my perfectly adequate stroller at a playgroup one afternoon, one mom looked inquisitively at me and finally asked if I had left my Bugaboo at home. I'm ashamed to admit it, but I actually found myself feeling embarrassed and could barely answer the question. Looking back, I wished I had said that I banked the extra $700 in my kid's college savings fund.

Having a plan, however, doesn't mean you can't ever splurge on things that are important to you. For instance, we decided to spend $450 for a professional photographer to come to our home and capture our seven-month-old's toothless grin. Sure, we could have spent a fraction of that on prints from a retailer's studio, but we wanted something more intimate and felt the cost was worth it. We had also budgeted for one extravagant item during our daughter's first year, so we knew we could afford to make this choice. For you that one extravagant thing might be the Bugaboo, having a baby nurse or throwing a lavish first-birthday party. The point is that this book is designed to give you the flexibility to choose your own indulgences while maintaining your family's financial security.

So for all of you parents who want to provide a secure fu-

ACTION PLAN FOR PARENTS

Don't have time to sit down and read this book from cover to cover? This ten-step game plan is a quick and handy reference to jump-start your family's finances.

1. Draft a will and name a guardian.
2. Draw up a trust and name a trustee.
3. Buy life insurance and consider a life insurance trust.
4. Track your spending and develop a family budget.
5. (Continue to) set aside money for retirement.
6. Take advantage of all tax-advantaged benefits at work (health care flexible spending account, dependent care account, etc.).
7. Take advantage of child-friendly tax credits and deductions.
8. Set up a college fund (only if you can afford it).
9. Set up a savings plans for other long-term goals, including a larger home.
10. Reassess your budget as your situation changes (additional kids, change in child care needs, etc.).

ture for your children but simply don't know where to start, *The Wall Street Journal. Financial Guidebook for New Parents* provides your road map. In these chapters, you'll receive a step-by-step plan for getting your family's finances in order that is relevant whether you are expecting, have an infant or have a handful of kids in elementary school or older.

This book is broken down into three sections. Part One, "When Baby Makes Three," helps readers make the financial transition from carefree individuals to parents.

Starting with the first chapter, "Your Maternity (or Paternity) Leave," I'll walk readers through the realities of maternity benefits. I'll explain to expectant parents how much

money they can count on from their employers and how to figure out how much time they can realistically afford to take off
for maternity leave.

Chapter 2, "Kissing That Cubicle Good-bye," discusses the
financial implications of staying home and caring for the children. Families need to realize that it isn't enough to simply
subtract the stay-at-home parent's paycheck; they also need to
consider the value of their previous corporate benefits, including health insurance and retirement plan. This section
will also discuss strategies to help stay-at-home parents work
part-time to help keep their foot in the door, and how to reenter the workforce once the kids start school.

Next, Chapter 3, "Returning to the Grind," uncovers the
financial pros and cons of returning to your job. On the positive side, it's nice to have that paycheck and the corporate benefits, especially the retirement account. But some parents may
find child care is so expensive that it actually costs them money
to go to work.

There's some good news in Chapter 4, "Who Says Uncle
Sam Doesn't Care?," where I'll explain all of the tax benefits
that come with children. While there are some pretty generous deductions and credits for the taking, families should be
aware that many of them start to phase out as couples hit certain income levels. I'll also discuss how the IRS handles divorce
and children.

Chapter 5, "Where Should You Nest?," tackles the "urban
or suburban" debate. Most couples find they want more space
when baby makes three. But a move from the city to the suburbs may not make as much financial sense as people think
once they factor in such extra costs as two cars and a commute.
Even the cost of upgrading to a larger home or a roomier car
can be more expensive than parents expect, once maintenance and gas are included in the equation.

In the second section, "No One Ever Said Kids Were Cheap,"
I'll discuss the major expenses associated with children.

I'll uncloak the cost of child care in Chapter 6, "Finding

(and Paying for) Mary Poppins." I'll also describe how to hire a nanny legally and protect yourself against litigation should your babysitter get injured on the job.

In Chapter 7, "Avoiding a Health Scare," I'll warn readers that they need to closely manage their health care and all of the related paperwork, or risk paying through the nose for each office visit and lab test. I'll show parents how they can strategize to stretch their health care dollars for the entire family.

What's often the biggest expense, education, is covered in Chapter 8, "Paying for Harvard." I'll tell readers just how much a university education will cost in eighteen years. I'll then show families the best ways to save this vast sum of money. I'll also help all those parents who are debating whether or not they should send their young children to private school.

Lastly, in Part Three, "Your Contingency Plan," I'll discuss four documents every family needs to protect themselves against the unthinkable.

First, in Chapter 9, "Yes, You Need a Will," I'll walk parents through the importance of drafting a will and naming a guardian. Here's a little secret: without this document a court will decide who cares for your children if both parents should pass away.

Once the will is set, Chapter 10, "Trusts: They Aren't Just for the Wealthy," will explain why most families should also set up a trust and name a trustee. Despite any preconceived notions you may have about trusts, they're a useful tool for middle-class parents or anyone who wants a say in how their assets will be spent on their children.

Chapter 11, "Life Insurance: Better Safe Than Sorry," takes the complexity out of buying life insurance. I'll demystify the difference between term and whole life and help you determine how much insurance you need.

Then I'll argue why most people should consider buying individual disability insurance in Chapter 12, "Accidents Happen . . . Are You Prepared?" The amount of coverage typically provided by an employer-sponsored plan falls short of covering an average family's expenses. The second half of the chapter will clarify what to look for in a policy and which riders are worth the extra money.

Finally, for all those parents looking for useful advice on how to save on everyday items, I've also included a special section, "Money-Saving Tips for Every Stage," from experienced parents who've already been there.

One of the biggest problems new parents face is that they don't see major expenses coming their way, and that leaves them unprepared to pay for them. This book will walk you through all the financial hits most parents with young children take, and it will help you fend them off. Remember, it's okay to feel a bit intimidated after a new child is born, but it's no time to ignore your finances in the hopes that they'll just work themselves out.

I won't lie to you. Having children is expensive. But with a little planning, you can raise your brood and still have enough left over for a comfortable retirement. This book will help you get there.

PART ONE

WHEN BABY MAKES THREE

CHAPTER 1

YOUR MATERNITY (OR PATERNITY) LEAVE

Common Misconception:

Maternity (or paternity) benefits are so generous that I can easily afford to take at least three months off to bond with my baby.

The Reality:

Most mothers receive six to eight weeks of disability payments, making maternity leave a financial strain during an already stressful time.

The Bottom Line:

It's up to you alone to make your maternity leave possible. Plan ahead and start building a reserve fund to help you afford all the time off that your employer allows.

ongratulations, you're pregnant!

Now brace yourself for some unwelcome news. Along with hemorrhoids and hormonal mood swings, meager maternity benefits are just one more harsh reality that no one warns pregnant women about.

Once you officially announce your good news to your boss, you'll quickly figure out that your time off with the baby could put a serious strain on your finances. Don't kid yourself— maternity leave is no paid vacation. While most companies try to paint themselves as "family-friendly," the reality is that most employers provide only the bare minimum in terms of benefits required by law. That means that if you work for a large company, you may get only twelve weeks of unpaid leave. If you're employed by a small firm, you may not get even that.

Even so, don't panic. The truth is that maternity leave is only the first of many financial challenges that will come your way as new parents. But along with learning how to change diapers and swaddle a newborn, you can master managing your money at this more complicated stage of your life, too. In this chapter I'll provide you with all of the information and tools you need to get through your maternity leave with your finances intact.

GET AN EARLY START

The best way to budget for your maternity leave is to start saving while you're still pregnant. With some careful planning and a bit of discipline, you should be able to afford to take as much time to bond with your baby as your employer allows. Let's take a closer look at how one couple, Jennifer and Steven Share, managed to do it.

When Jennifer was pregnant with her first child, she worked as a CPA for a small accounting firm in New Jersey. Her employer was generous and offered all of its female employees six months of maternity leave. Although the time off was unpaid, Jennifer managed to take full advantage of this benefit and bond with her baby without derailing the family's finances.

What was her secret? Before Jennifer got pregnant she found out how much time her company would allow her to spend with a baby. She then started setting aside a little money

THREE STEPS TO FIGURING OUT HOW MUCH YOU'LL NEED

Fortunately, you don't need to be an accountant like Jennifer to figure out how to afford a full maternity leave. These three steps will help you get there.

Step 1: Find Out How Much Leave You Get and If Any of It's Paid

As soon as you announce you're expecting, go to your human resources department and find out how much maternity leave you're entitled to and how much money you'll see during those weeks off. (See page 13 for more on what employers are legally required to provide.) Armed with this information, you'll know exactly how much cash is coming in while you're taking care of your new baby.

Step 2: Crunch the Numbers and Figure Out How Much Money You'll Need

Track your current spending and compare your total monthly expenses to your cash flow during the unpaid portion of your leave. This exercise will tell you where your new family stands financially. (The worksheet on page 186 in the Appendix can help you get started.) If you're like many young, two-income households, there's a good chance you'll find yourselves initially coming up short without that extra paycheck. Don't despair. Just write down exactly how much you need to help cover your expenses, and then I'll show you some easy ways to help bridge the gap in your budget.

Step 3: Find Ways to Save Money So You Can Afford to Take a Full Leave

Now it's time to come up with a savings plan to help make up for that lost paycheck. When you fill out the spending worksheet you'll notice that expenses are broken down into two categories: basic necessities and extraneous items. These extraneous items, including entertainment, shopping and daily trips to Starbucks, are your opportunities to save money each month without much sacrifice on your part. Also remember to factor in the expenses that disappear when you're not working, such as commuting and dry cleaning. If you're still in the red, you're going to have to find some more aggressive ways to spend less. (For ideas on how to do this, see page 16.)

each month in a reserve fund to help pay bills once the couple lost her paycheck during maternity leave.

But soon after Jennifer conceived that plan hit a snag. Steven lost his job and the couple felt what it was like to live on just one salary a lot sooner than they had planned. "I was in panic mode," Jennifer says. At that point the Shares realized that they needed a safety net that was large enough to carry them should they both be out of work at the same time.

A couple of months later, Steven found a new job and Jennifer started saving much more aggressively. "I wanted to bank six months of mortgage payments," she says. Fortunately for the Shares, Jennifer reached her savings goal a little early; a difficult pregnancy forced her to stop working six weeks before her due date and put her on disability.

Looking back, Jennifer admits it was tough to cut back their spending before her daughter was born. But once she arrived, Jennifer and Steven knew the sacrifice was worth it. There's nothing Jennifer would have traded in exchange for those precious six months with her baby girl.

No matter what you do, don't let your maternity leave set you up for a financial setback later on. While it may be tempting to live off your credit cards for a little while, the reality is that your expenses will only increase

PATERNITY LEAVE

What about dads? They're allowed to take time off to bond with the baby, too. Under the FMLA, men who work for a large employer or a public agency are entitled to twelve weeks of unpaid leave. David Leibowitz, an attorney and father of three, took full advantage of the law. When his first child arrived he took three months off from the Middlesex District Attorney's office in Cambridge, Massachusetts, to care for his daughter after his wife went back to work. "It was the greatest experience of my life," he says. He has since taken a formal leave after the birth of each of his children.

Financially speaking, it would be very tough for most young couples to survive without any money coming in for three months. Instead, many fathers save up their vacation and use that time off to help with a new child.

once a baby arrives, making it more difficult to chip away at the debt over time.

HOW MUCH TIME YOU'LL GET TO SPEND WITH YOUR BABY

Under the Family and Medical Leave Act of 1993 (FMLA), public agencies and employers with at least fifty employees are required to give new parents only twelve weeks of unpaid leave. Some states, however, have passed similar laws that may apply to women who aren't given time off under the federal law. (Contact your state's Department of Labor to figure out how much time your employer is required to provide for maternity leave.) Your firm, like Jennifer Share's, may also opt to provide you with a longer leave.

Now for the bad news. If you're like the 45 percent of workers who receive a paycheck from a small company with fewer than fifty employees, you won't fall under the protection of the FMLA. That means you aren't entitled to twelve weeks off to recover from the birth itself and bond with your baby. But if your company has at least fifteen employees, your boss must offer you the same insurance and any other support it provides other workers with medical or disability leave under the Pregnancy Discrimination Act.

FIGHTING PREGNANCY DISCRIMINATION

Can't imagine your boss would treat you differently simply because you're expecting? Think again. Pregnancy discrimination is actually on the rise and is the fastest-growing type of discrimination in the workforce, according to the U.S. Equal Employment Opportunity Commission (EEOC). In fiscal year 2007, the EEOC received 5,587 charges of pregnancy-based discrimination. It resolved 4,979 of those charges and recovered $30 million in monetary benefits. For more details on the Pregnancy Discrimination Act or to file a complaint, contact the U.S. Equal Employment Opportunity Commission (EEOC) or check out its Web site at eeoc.gov.

HOW MUCH MONEY YOU CAN EXPECT DURING YOUR LEAVE

The most important question most families have is how much Mom will get paid during her maternity leave. (Paternity leave, however, is unpaid under the FMLA.) Unfortunately, the federal law doesn't require employers to pay you anything during your time off. Many companies, however, do have short-term disability insurance for their employees. If that's the case, you can probably count on six weeks of disability for a vaginal delivery or eight weeks for a cesarean, plus any accrued vacation you've already earned. In some cases you may also be able to tap into your sick days.

ADOPTION AND FOSTER BENEFITS

Parents who adopt or foster a child are entitled to twelve weeks of unpaid leave under the FMLA. Although companies are not required to provide any financial assistance, more are starting to do so. In 2007, 47 percent of major U.S. companies offered their employees monetary assistance toward adoption, according to human resources consulting firm Hewitt Associates. That's a big improvement from 1990, when just 12 percent did. The average firm that offers benefits gives its adoptive parents $5,000 and five weeks' paid leave, according to the Dave Thomas Foundation for Adoption.

Sounds pretty good, right? Before you decide to skip this chapter thinking you won't need to save any money before the baby arrives, realize that there's a slim chance disability pay will mirror your regular paycheck. That's because most disability payments are capped at between 50 percent and 60 percent of your salary. If you're adopting or fostering a child, you won't see any disability checks or sick leave (see sidebar).

So what will this mean for your budget? Let's say you get six weeks of disability payments, at 50 percent of your regular salary, and two weeks of paid vacation. That works out to the equivalent of a full paycheck for just five weeks. If you get three months off, you'll have to find a way to cover your expenses for the next seven weeks without Mom's income.

Contact your human resources department to find out exactly how much money you'll pull in during your leave and to get all the paperwork needed to apply for disability benefits. Your employer cannot fill out the forms on your behalf.

SAVING FOR YOUR MATERNITY LEAVE

My very generous employer allowed six months off for maternity leave, and I fortunately did not have to worry about money during the first two months. That's because money was still coming in the door thanks to my disability insurance and vacation—but I still had four months without any income that I needed to plan for.

Looking back, it was relatively easy to stash away at least part of the money we needed without even trying. While I was pregnant, I followed my doctor's orders and skipped drinks with colleagues after work. On the weekends, I was simply too tired to socialize as much as I used to. And once our daughter arrived, our social calendar came to a standstill. We didn't go out to eat or spend any money on entertainment for at least four months, other than the occasional Chinese takeout and Netflix DVDs.

Still, social hibernation alone probably won't save you enough to entirely make up for that lost paycheck. You'll need to be more proactive and somehow find ways to save money and set it aside for when the baby arrives. Saving for maternity leave is also just the beginning, and many of the steps you take now to afford the time off will also pay off after your baby is born. If you're having trouble figuring out how to save enough for maternity leave, maybe you need to take more drastic measures that will enable you to better afford your new bundle of joy once she arrives.

Remember the Shares? The first time around they managed to slash their budget by cutting back on frivolous shopping and entertainment. A few years later, when Jennifer was about to give birth to their third and fourth children (twin girls), they realized they needed to find more extreme ways to afford the cost of raising four kids. They decided to sell their house near the New Jersey shore and move to a cheaper neighborhood, decreasing their mortgage payment by $400 a month. They also bought a less expensive SUV, lowering their car payment by $60 a month.

There are literally hundreds of ways to save money. Here are just a few tips to help you get started and build up a reserve fund before your maternity leave. (See the full "Money-Saving Tips for Every Stage" guide at the end of the book for more ideas on how to cut back your child-related expenses.)

Save More

- **Consolidate your debt.** Don't waste money on high-interest-rate credit cards. Instead, transfer your balances to a zero-percent or low-interest-rate card and then aggressively work toward paying off what you owe. This will help free up cash flow both during maternity leave and after the baby arrives.

- **Cut back on eating out.** You can easily slash your spending by doing some simple things like bringing your lunch to work (if you save $3 a day, that will total $60 a month) or drinking the office decaf instead of splurging on a $3.50 cup of joe from Starbucks ($70 a month).

- **Downsize your entertainment costs.** Skip your weekly trip to the movie theater and rent a DVD instead and you can save up to $70 a month. When that's not enough, get creative and consider inviting friends over for game night rather than dining out at an expensive restaurant.

- **Audit your utilities and other household bills.** While nesting, make a list of household services, such as premium cable channels, that you're not using and cancel them. Consider dropping your landline and relying solely on your cell phone. If you want to keep your home phone, check out consumer Web sites such as LowerMyBills.com or MyRatePlan. com to see if there is a better service plan for you. You can even save hundreds a year by reducing your energy costs if you seal leaky windows and use Energy Star appliances.

Spend Less

- **Avoid the urge to upgrade.** Just because a baby is on the way doesn't mean you need to sell a reliable (and affordable) car and get a new SUV. As long as you have a backseat with room for an infant seat, you're set.

- **Hold off on the McMansion.** There's no reason to rush moving into a larger and more costly home. Provided there's room in your current house for a crib, you should be fine. It's better to wait until you've figured out what your future finances will look like before you start increasing your financial commitments. One of the biggest dangers is that you could buy a new house based on two paychecks only to realize later that one of you wants to stay home with the baby.

- **Register for as much as possible.** A common error expectant parents make is spending hundreds of dollars on baby items before the birth only to be inundated with gifts at a shower or after the little one's arrival. Instead, register for the items you need, and wait and see what you get.

- **Borrow from friends.** So much baby gear, including infant swings and bouncy seats, has a limited shelf life. If you plan to use an item for only a few months, try to borrow one from a friend. Not only do most parents want to help out, but they also realize that lending gear is a great way to get rid of large plastic objects until they have their next kid.

WHAT HAPPENS AFTER LEAVE?

Once your leave is up, you'll have to decide whether to go back to work or stay home with the baby. Most parents who plan to return to the workforce simply go back after their official leave is up. However, that's not what happened to Lia Gravier.

After taking three months off to care for her baby, Lia was ready to return to her job as the public relations manager at a New York City–based museum. Three days before she was scheduled to go back to work, her boss called her at home. The director of the museum told her he had given her her management position to someone else and that she could come back as a colleague's assistant.

Lia says she never saw the demotion coming. She had been in touch with her coworkers during her maternity leave and her boss never gave her any indication that her job was at risk. She was so taken aback by the phone call that she didn't initially know how to respond. She also wasn't entirely clear on what her rights were under the FMLA. After speaking with a lawyer, Lia learned that the FMLA guarantees that you can't be demoted while out on maternity leave; your employer must either hold your position for you or provide you one with equivalent benefits, pay, working conditions *and* seniority.

Although Lia initially considered filing a complaint against the museum, she later decided not to follow through. "You've just had this amazing thing happen in your life. Why turn it into something negative?" Lia quickly found a new job in a more family-friendly environment. She even managed to find a position where she could work part-time.

In the next two chapters, I'll help you decide what to do after your leave and discuss how your decision will affect your family financially over both the short term and the long haul. The good news is that having a financial game plan in place before your leave starts you off on the right financial foot, so you should be able to afford to raise your kids however you want, whether that's as a stay-at-home parent or as one who works in an office.

KNOW YOUR RIGHTS UNDER FMLA

 If your employer violates the FMLA, you can and should file a complaint with the secretary of labor by contacting your local Wage and Hour Division of the Employment Standards Administration, U.S. Department of Labor. If the Labor Department believes your complaint has merit, it will try to resolve the issue directly with your employer. In some cases, the secretary of labor may file a lawsuit on your behalf. If you win, you may get lost wages, employment benefits and possibly reinstatement of your job or even a promotion.

You should also know that there are certain circumstances where you could legitimately find yourself on the unemployment line. If your company is going through a reorganization—and what company isn't these days?—you could legally get the sack or be demoted while you're out on leave. Also, highly compensated women are at particular risk. Those who rank among the top 10 percent of highest-paid employees won't fall under the protection of the FMLA if a firm can argue that not having you around during your maternity leave will cause it serious economic injury.

If you lose your job while out on maternity leave, you'll also lose your health benefits. But don't panic if your family counts on this insurance. You may be eligible for COBRA, which means your former employer must keep you on its health plan for eighteen months but is no longer required to pay a portion of your premium. You'll be responsible for the entire bill, which averages $1,050 (for family coverage) a month. (The one exception is if you're laid off between September 1, 2008, and December 31, 2009. You may be eligible for a 65 percent government subsidy for nine months toward your premiums.) While this may sound pricey, some families find that it's still a relative bargain compared with comprehensive health insurance options sold on the private market. (I'll discuss health insurance and money-saving strategies in Chapter 7.)

For more information on the Family and Medical Leave Act, check out the Department of Labor's Web site at dol.gov.

CHAPTER 2

KISSING THAT CUBICLE GOOD-BYE

> ### Common Misconception:
> If I quit my job, all I lose is my paycheck, which would probably get eaten by child care anyway.
>
> ### The Reality:
> Walk away from a corporate job and you also lose attractive benefits such as affordable health insurance, a retirement account and a flexible spending account, which allows you to use pretax dollars for health care and child care expenses.
>
> ### The Bottom Line:
> Make sure to factor in your salary plus the cost of benefits when deciding if your family can afford to live on just one income.

I s your baby smiling and sleeping for longer stretches through the night? Then chances are your leave is almost over and you have a big decision to make. Will you or your spouse stay home and raise your little one full-time or will you go back to work?

Don't underestimate how difficult this decision can be. Some of the most successful executives feel torn between their love for their new babies and their careers. Indeed, more and more mothers are opting to stay home. According to the U.S. Bureau of Labor Statistics, 47 percent of married women with infants stay home with their babies, nearly a six-percentage-point increase since 1997. And of those women who return to their jobs, nearly 32 percent of them work part-time.

While the decision to raise children full-time is often made with the heartstrings, this chapter will discuss why you also need to consider the purse strings. There's no right or wrong way to raise a child, but the choices you make have real financial implications. Figuring them out now allows you to adjust your budget and lifestyle accordingly.

Consider this: when you give up your job, you're not simply saying good-bye to your paycheck. In the short term, you're also losing valuable benefits, including corporate-sponsored health insurance and the ability to make contributions toward Social Security, a tax-deferred retirement account and a flexible spending account that allows you to put pretax dollars toward health care and child care expenses. In the long term, a stay-at-home parent also gives up his or her full earning potential since you're likely to face a cut in both position and pay when you do decide to return to the workforce. (I'll talk more about how you can strategically navigate time off a little later in the chapter.)

Having said all that, there's no need to second-guess your decision to stay home just yet and rush back to the nine-to-five grind. While it's difficult to imagine life beyond a feeding and nap schedule, in just a few short years your child will enter kindergarten and you'll be either juggling additional kids or deciding it's time to return to the workforce. Either way, there are things you can do now that can make that transition easier.

FIGURE OUT WHAT YOU'RE IN FOR

Before your leave is over, think about what it would be like to spend all of your time with a baby. Will you be happy filling your days with Mommy and Me groups and music classes? Just

THREE STEPS FOR THE STAY-AT-HOME PARENT

This simple three-step plan will help you figure out if being a stay-at-home mom or dad is the right decision for your family. If it is, I'll walk you through ways to make it more affordable.

Step 1:
Do the Math

Now that you've lived through the drama of your leave, you should have a pretty good idea of what your day-to-day expenditures look like with a baby and if you can afford to live on just one salary. Track your current spending and crunch the numbers one last time. Make sure you take into account any expenses, such as health care, that may increase once you lose your work-related benefits.

Step 2:
Create a Long-Term Budget

Now it's time to update the budget you created for your leave. (Or create one if you didn't previously have one.) During your leave you were simply trying to make it through a short period of time on one salary. Now you need a sustainable spending plan that will not only allocate money for daily expenses but also set aside funds for long-term goals, including retirement, insurance premiums and, if you can afford it, college savings. (The Monthly Budgeting Worksheet in the Appendix can help you.)

Step 3:
Have a Reentry Plan

Many parents who choose to stay home with their children eventually want to return to the workforce. While some may miss the challenging work and camaraderie they felt in an office, others simply need the money. Whatever the reason, now is the time to keep your network vibrant and plan your reentry. I'll show you how to do this later on in the chapter.

as important, can you afford to walk away from your job? Did you, for example, struggle living on just one salary right after your child was born? Or was it easier than you imagined? Many families find that they're able to live on just one income, provided they make some changes to their lifestyle. We'll meet two families later in this chapter who have successfully found a way for one parent to stay home and who say the financial sacrifice was well worth the opportunity to spend more time raising their children.

CAN YOU AFFORD TO STAY HOME?

If you thought budgeting for your leave was difficult, just wait until you try to permanently go from two salaries to one. If it turns out you'll have to start living paycheck to paycheck and no longer have money left over at the end of the month for savings, you may want to rethink your decision. At the very least, you may want to put a limit on the amount of time you'll go without a paycheck, figure out a way to work part-time or decide you'll go back to work once your youngest reaches kindergarten.

In some circumstances, families may actually find it more expensive for a parent with a very small child or two kids to go back to work once the cost of child care is factored in. I'll talk more about this and other work-related expenses in Chapter 3.

As I mentioned earlier, you can't simply subtract your paycheck to budget for life on one salary. If your family has been depending on your health insurance, for example, you could see a marked increase in your premiums if you switch to your spouse's plan or have to buy coverage on the open market. New mother Tawnya Stone learned how valuable her employer-sponsored benefits were the hard way. When she switched to her husband's insurance plan after deciding to stay home with her baby, she was shocked to watch her premium increase ten-fold. The Stones went from paying less than $100 a month to

$1,000 for a plan that offered less coverage. Don't let yourself be caught unaware in a similar situation.

You also can't forget to put a value on your retirement account. Let's say you were making $60,000 and contributing 10 percent of it annually into a 401(k). Now let's say your company offered a match of 3 percent and that the value of your account grew at a conservative 6 percent. In thirty years, your retirement account would have grown to over $600,000 if you'd remained at your job. (Stay-at-home parents can contribute to a spousal IRA, which I'll discuss a little later on in the chapter.)

On the positive side, by staying home with your child, you won't have to pay for pricey child care, a burden that breaks many working parents' budgets, especially if you have more than one kid.

On page 183 you'll find the Working Versus Staying Home Worksheet to help you figure out the true financial impact of your decision to raise your baby full-time. To get a realistic comparison, do the research and find out how much child care costs in your area.

SETTING YOUR BUDGET

If you've decided to stay home, it's time to face your finances head-on. Fortunately, creating a spending plan isn't as hard as it sounds. It will also help you prioritize and manage your cash flow, so you'll avoid digging into your savings. First, start out by listing all of your fixed expenses. If you look at the Monthly Budgeting Worksheet on page 186, you'll see these include your mortgage (or rent), utilities, insurance, taxes, food, car payments, commuting expenses and any debt, including student loans and credit card bills. Now, list all of the new costs associated with the baby, including clothing, diapers and formula. Add it all up and compare it to the family's new monthly after-tax income to see how much you will have left over. (See? Wasn't that simple?)

THE EMOTIONAL COST OF STAYING HOME

Having a baby is an emotional adjustment for any couple. But that change can feel even more dramatic when one parent decides to stay home with the baby.

Amy Fisher, a former computer programmer, says leaving the workforce was a more difficult transition than she anticipated. Learning to care for her daughter was manageable. The challenging part was that she felt her marriage suddenly became very traditional. "It really changes the playing field a lot when you're not contributing anything [financially]. I felt as if I lost independence I didn't even know I had."

Fortunately, things got easier for the couple after the first few months. Amy was able to bring their marriage back into balance by talking through her issues with her husband. It turns out that while Amy felt she had lost some power in her marriage since she was no longer contributing a paycheck, her husband didn't share that opinion and valued what she did very much.

Two years later—and with a second new baby at home—Amy believes she made the right decision to stop working. While she may not be making direct deposits into a joint checking account, she feels more in control of her life and that her work raising two kids is priceless.

Now that you've accounted for your basic necessities, the remaining cash needs to be split between your elective expenses (including entertainment, shopping and babysitters) and your savings goals, most importantly your retirement.

Here's where things can get tricky. Many couples feel like there isn't enough money left over after paying their fixed expenses. This isn't so surprising considering your family income just dropped when one parent decided to stay home and your overall expenses increased thanks to the new little one.

> ## BUDGETING FOR ONE WILL HELP YOU BUDGET FOR MORE
>
> While you may initially spend less on a second child since you already have a lot of the infant gear, including a crib and changing table, expenses will soon catch up and you'll eventually end up spending about the same amount on each kid. So keeping track of your current baby-related spending now will help you figure out how many children you can afford later.

When faced with this cash crunch, the biggest mistake new parents make is that they stop setting aside money for their retirement. Understandably, in the short term, this feels like the least painful way to find extra money for daily expenses. After all, you can enjoy watching your little girl play with her new Leap Frog learning table now, or you can stash that $40 into a retirement account that you won't need for another thirty-five years. The problem is that you will need a rather large sum of money to live on during your retirement. If you put off saving for that goal until your kids are older, you may find that you can't stop working and earning until long after age sixty-five, a sad reality many baby boomers are now facing.

FINDING EXTRA MONEY

Most young families throw away hundreds of dollars a month without even realizing it. Let's start with all those baby-related items you think you *must* have. Clearly, you can't cut back on the baby formula or medical expenses. But there's no reason your child needs a nursery outfitted by Pottery Barn Kids or a wardrobe by the pricey French clothing company Bonpoint. And other than perishable food, you'll be hard pressed to find anything in your home with a shorter shelf life than baby and toddler gear. Your kid will outgrow an outfit in a matter of months and grow bored with a toy before the batteries wear out. That's why I recommend choosing the cheapest items you can (without sacrificing safety) and borrowing as many things as possible from friends.

When my daughter was born, we bought a new crib and car seat, since experts warn of dangers associated with buying these items used. We then borrowed everything else we could get our hands on, from a swing and Gymini activity mat to a breast-feeding pillow and infant Snap-N-Go stroller. The rest of the nursery was outfitted with used items we found on Craigslist. We were able, for example, to get a glider that retails for $500 for just $100. It *is* possible to get the baby items you most need and want for less.

Next, take a look at how much you're spending. As I mentioned in the previous chapter, even cutting out the convenience of buying your lunch rather than bringing it from home can save you around $100 a month. Consider Beth Stalter, a former teacher, and her husband, who works in finance, who realized while Beth was out on maternity leave that eating at restaurants and getting takeout was costing them up to $600 a month. By cooking at home most nights, the Stalters now save $400 a month and still manage to go out for a regular "date night." The money they save goes toward their retirement and a 529 college savings plan.

Finally, as we touched on in the last chapter, you may find that you need to lower some of your fixed expenses to allow yourselves more breathing room. After all, having kids is stressful enough without always worrying about money.

Tawnya Stone, the same mom who was shocked to learn how much her health insurance costs increased when she switched to her husband's plan, decided along with her husband that moving might be the remedy to the stresses of living on less. When Tawnya, a project manager, had her first child, she and her husband, who's a teacher, lived in Washington, D.C., and earned a combined salary of about $150,000 a year. Soon after they had their daughter, Tawnya decided to quit her job and stay home. The family's income dropped to just $50,000. The couple knew they had to dramatically decrease their spending, and that led them back home to Iowa. Tawnya says the family's living expenses are considerably lower than they were in Washington, D.C. (primarily because of real estate prices), making it relatively easy to live comfortably on an educator's salary. For more ideas on ways to cut fixed costs, refer back to page 16.

RETIREMENT

So how much should you be saving for retirement? As a general rule, individuals should sock away at least 10 percent of their income. Here's the rub: if both you and your spouse were working before you had a baby and one of you decides to stay home, you've just slashed about half your savings by walking away from that job. Since your needs during your golden years haven't changed, the nonworking spouse still needs to try to set aside as much money as before for retirement.

Enter the spousal IRA. Recognizing that nonworking spouses are at a disadvantage, the IRS allows many stay-at-home parents the opportunity to contribute to a tax-advantaged account. If you file a joint tax return, a nonworking spouse can make a $5,000 tax-deductible contribution into an IRA, provided the working spouse has enough earned income to cover the contribution. The one exception to the rule is for couples making over $176,000—unfortunately, they are not eligible for the spousal IRA.

DO YOU QUALIFY FOR A SPOUSAL IRA?

Uncle Sam doesn't let all families contribute to a spousal IRA. If one spouse is covered by a qualified retirement plan (through either your employer or self-employment), then your right to make a deductible contribution into a spousal IRA phases out if the family's adjusted gross income is between $166,000 and $176,000. If, however, neither spouse is covered by a 401(k) or some other qualifying retirement plan, both of you can make a $5,000 deductible contribution into an IRA, regardless of your income. (The rules are slightly different for folks age fifty and older.) For more information, visit the IRS Web site at irs.gov.

RETURNING TO THE WORKFORCE

Remember all those annoying secrets about pregnancy that no one tells you until you conceive, such as the linea nigra, the dark line some women develop on their bellies? Well, staying at home has a few of its own undisclosed zingers, too. Topping the list, it's more difficult to return to the workforce after a stint at home than most women anticipate. And even those who do it successfully complain that they had to take a cut in salary and position to make it happen.

Nearly 40 percent of highly qualified women opt out of the workforce to care for either children or elderly parents, according to economist Sylvia Ann Hewlett's book *Off-Ramps and On-Ramps: Keeping Talented Women on the Road to Success*. Ninety-three percent of these women eventually want to return to work, but only 74 percent of them succeed. And of those, only 40 percent are able to secure full-time positions. If those statistics aren't discouraging enough, women who take two years off find that they're penalized by losing 18 percent of their earning power. Stay home for three years or more, and the average salary drops 37 percent.

Fortunately, there are simple things you can do—starting as early as when you announce your departure to your manager—that can help ease your transition back into the workforce, even if your return is years away.

WHAT YOU CAN DO NOW

Keep working. Tory Johnson, the founder and CEO of Women for Hire, recommends never cutting yourself off entirely from the working world. During your exit interview, for example, tell your manager that your time off is only temporary and that you're open to project work or freelance assignments. By consulting a few hours a week or even just a few months out of the year, you're keeping your contacts fresh and your resume up to date.

Maintain your network. While there's no need to remain on top of the latest corner-office gossip, you should try to maintain your network and schedule regular lunches with former colleagues. At the very least, stay in e-mail contact. Also, make sure to send all of your professional contacts holiday cards. When you're ready to return to work, these are the people who will be in the best position to either hire you or recommend you for a new position.

Stay current. Consider joining a professional organization and attending meetings and other events at least twice a year. Not only will you stay current with your chosen industry, but you can also expand your network and meet decision makers within your profession. If you can't attend gatherings, at the very least read the group's newsletters and any other trade publications you can get your hands on.

WHAT YOU CAN DO LATER

Reach out. Get the word out. As soon as you start thinking about returning to work, tell everyone in your network that you're looking for a job. If you want to change industries, start working your network of friends and neighbors. Even if many of your friends are also staying at home, their spouses and acquaintances may be able to help you. The important thing is that you're very clear about what you're looking for. For example, if you know that you want to work in advertising sales, be sure to ask everyone you know if they have contacts in newspaper, magazine or online publishing as well as television.

Meet key decision makers. Don't waste all of your time surfing online job boards. Web ads tend to attract so many candidates that a hiring manager is likely to discard any resume with a gap, says Johnson. Your better bet is to get face-to-face with as many people as possible by requesting informational interviews. Once you're sitting with a hiring manager, you'll have a much better chance at convincing him or her that you'd be an asset to the organization. And he or she is more likely to remember you and call you back when a job does become available.

Prepare for tough questions. Don't be surprised if potential employers question your commitment to returning to the workforce. "The biggest questions you'll need to answer are why now and why me," Johnson says. The best answer you can give is that you've always planned to return to work, you've given this a lot of thought and you feel confident that now is the right time for you. And most importantly, mention that you've already lined up your child care, so you're ready to start right away.

GET YOUR FOOT IN THE DOOR

Take it slow. "The reality is that when you take time off, time doesn't freeze," says Johnson. "You don't just take off and return to exactly where you were in position, pay and even opportunity." Unfortunately, you may have to take a lesser job or even a part-time or freelance position to start rebuilding your professional reputation. That's why Johnson recommends that stay-at-home parents consider taking a part-time assignment a year or two before they ideally want to reenter the workforce in a full-time capacity.

That's just what Renee Teich, a speech therapist with two kids, did. When her youngest was three, she started working a few hours a week while her child was in preschool. Although she wasn't thinking of returning to full-time work in the near future, she considered the job an opportunity to get back into the field after staying home for six years.

What Renee didn't know at the time was that she would end up getting divorced just a couple of years later and would need to return to full-time work sooner than she had planned. Fortunately, her part-time work had allowed her to maintain her strong reputation in her field and community, and she didn't struggle with finding a new job. In Renee's case, that part-time work in her daughter's elementary school turned into a full-time position that also means she can still be home for her children when school lets out.

Ultimately, you have to find a way to make your finances work with the way you decide to raise your child. If transitioning back into the workforce after being gone for an extended period seems too daunting, or if living on one salary turns out not to be the right move for your family, the next chapter helps parents know what to expect when they decide to go back to work as soon as their leave is up.

CHAPTER 3

RETURNING TO THE GRIND

Common Misconception:
As long as both parents work, raising children won't strain the family budget.

The Reality:
Child care is pricey. Don't expect those paychecks to stretch nearly as far as they used to.

The Bottom Line:
Figure out how much after-tax money is left over in the family budget after child care and plan accordingly. And make sure you exploit every benefit your employer offers to help stretch your paycheck.

So you decided after Chapter 2 that you need to go back to work, that you love your career too much not to or that you'll simply go bonkers if you attend one more Mommy and Me luncheon. You're not alone: despite the trend of more women and men opting out of the workforce or staying home during the day, the majority of new parents do return to the working world. And if you're heading back to the grind, you want to make sure you structure your work situation and take full advantage of all of the perks to best meet your family's needs.

What are some of those perks? In addition to a paycheck, employees also get access to a tax-advantaged retirement account and more affordable health insurance. And many companies provide their workers with the ability to set aside pretax dollars for health and child care expenses. Not to be forgotten is that by staying in the workforce, parents also maximize their future earning potential.

Gabrielle Rosenfeld, a corporate researcher from Riverdale, New York, admits that she struggled with her decision regarding whether to go back to work. Right around the time she had her son, she also completed her master's degree in library research. She knew she wanted to put her degree to use and keep her proverbial foot in the professional world; she worried that taking time off with her son would hurt her long-term earning potential. On the other hand, Gabrielle was raised by a stay-at-home mother and greatly enjoyed the special time the two of them spent together after school. She wanted the same for her son.

Entirely conflicted, Gabrielle and her husband, Joe, decided to run the numbers and see how their finances would look under both scenarios. While the Rosenfelds didn't need Gabrielle's salary to put food on the table, her paycheck would make their lives a bit more comfortable and allow them to indulge their son in music classes and other enrichment programs without putting a strain on their budget.

In the end, the decision was made when—after a couple of months at home—Gabrielle realized she wanted to go back to work. "I'm a better parent when I also have the opportunity to be an adult for part of the day," she says. She believes her son benefits, too. "My kid's life is richer because he has other relationships in his life."

WORKING MAKES SENSE

What do you do if you want to return to work but discover that you're handing over most or all of your after-tax paycheck to

THREE STEPS FOR RETURNING TO WORK

If you decide to go back to work, these simple steps will help ensure that you get the most from your time away from home.

Step 1: Crunch the Numbers

If you skipped Chapter 2 because you never considered staying home, turn to the Working Versus Staying Home Worksheet on page 183 and run your budget through it. Make sure you can afford to pay for child care, and get a feel for how your money will be spent.

Step 2: Negotiate Your Terms

The good news is that companies are more flexible than ever. Don't think that you necessarily have to decide between staying home and working sixty hours a week. If you're a valued employee, your company may be open to you working part-time or telecommuting a few days a week. The key is to set up your new terms of employment before your maternity leave is over. You could also look for a new job that is more open to flexible hours.

Step 3: Use Every Benefit Your Employer Offers

No matter what you decide, the reality is that having a child comes with a slew of new expenses. You need to make sure that you're taking advantage of every possible corporate benefit your company offers, including flexible spending accounts for health care and child care, so that you're maximizing the value you're getting from working. This will also help you stretch your paycheck farther.

your child's caregiver? Many parents might be tempted to resign on the spot. After all, what's the point of working if you aren't making any money? But most career and financial experts would argue that you're still better off in the long term if you stay in the workforce now.

If your salary doesn't stretch much beyond child care today, it could tomorrow. Walk away from your job and you're missing the opportunity for raises and promotions. Keep in mind that if you plan to eventually return to the workforce, you're likely to have to take a cut in pay and position when you do, and that will have a severe impact on your future earning potential.

Even if money isn't an issue today, it could be later on. You never know what life may throw your way. There's always the chance that the working spouse could get laid off, become disabled or pass away, or that the relationship itself could end through divorce and the nonworking spouse would be forced to reenter the workforce. At the risk of stating the obvious, transitioning back into the working world, especially during an already difficult time in your life, is a lot harder than never having left it at all.

Finally, having two working spouses also provides families with more financial flexibility. When Samantha Lau and Alan Wang were about to have their first child, Alan worked at a software company and his job required constant travel. If he continued on in that job, he would have barely seen his son and Samantha would have been burdened with the majority of the child care responsibilities.

Instead, the couple decided they wanted a more balanced family life. Alan quit his job and decided to work for himself investing in real estate. He is now pursuing his passion and can take an active role in raising his two kids. Alan was able to do all this only because Samantha, who works in finance, receives health insurance through her employer. Her steady paycheck also balances out Alan's less predictable income.

NEGOTIATE YOUR TERMS

As I mentioned earlier, after I had my daughter, I was able to return to work part-time and have the best of both worlds: spend more time with my baby and still keep my hand in the workforce. I was fortunate because many of my friends didn't have the option to return to their jobs in a limited fashion.

My good luck was due to the fact my employer has a policy that new mothers are allowed to return to work on a part-time basis for up to five years. Each supervisor, however, has some discretion over an employee's hours. Over time, my workload increased and I needed to spend more hours in the office to get everything done. Had I refused the additional assignments, I might have put my part-time status in jeopardy.

Pat Katepoo, founder of WorkOptions.com, believes that working flexible hours is a growing trend and that even if your employer doesn't have a formal part-time policy, you may be able to negotiate a deal for yourself. The key is to create a written proposal allowing for a six-month trial period for your supervisor long before you go out on maternity leave. Katepoo recommends the proposal define what you do now, which reinforces your value, and how you would structure your new role. You should also explain what elements of your job would need to be shared or delegated to other people.

Next, the proposal should answer the two most common protests bosses make. The first one: the company has no official policy. Respond by stating that allowing part-time schedules is an effective productivity tool used by thousands of companies. Then list firms in your industry that allow flexible hours. You can find examples in *Working Mother* magazine's annual 100 Best Companies survey. The second: supervisors often fear that if they let one parent in the office work part-time, everyone else will follow suit. You can reassure them that very few people choose part-time work since they can't afford the pay cut.

Finally, if you still can't get your supervisor to agree to a part-time schedule, try asking if you can telecommute one or two days a week, recommends Katepoo. The hours you're not spending in a car or on a train to the office will allow you to spend more time with your new baby. That worked for Gabrielle Rosenfeld, who negotiated the right to telecommute from

PART-TIME WORK CAN COST YOU PERKS

If you decide to work part-time, don't be surprised if you lose most of your corporate benefits. In some cases, employees need to meet a certain minimum number of hours a week to qualify for benefits. So make sure to check in with your human resources department to avoid missing out on a valuable perk such as health insurance just because you're a couple of hours shy of the requirement.

home two days a week. While she still needs child care while she's working from home, she can eat lunch with her son and doesn't have to waste precious time commuting.

Even if you can't telecommute, you may still be able to "extend" your leave by working part-time for a few months after you return. If a company wants to keep you, it will be creative in how it lets you work.

If your employer isn't flexible, look for another company that is. (Again, consult *Working Mother* magazine for family-friendly firms across the country.) Plenty of people switch jobs after having a child in favor of finding work closer to home or an opportunity that offers more flexible hours. Just don't quit your current job before you have something else lined up, if you depend on the income to make ends meet.

EXPLOITING ALL OF THE BENEFITS OF WORKING

Normally, companies allow you to make changes to your benefits just once a year. The one exception is when you've experienced a major life change, such as having a baby. So make sure you check in with your human resources department to find out what benefits you can adjust (think health insurance) and what new perks you may be eligible for, including a flexible spending account for dependent care.

Once parents earn what's considered an upper-middle-class income, they start to lose many family-friendly tax breaks.

But no matter how much you make, you can still take advantage of the following benefits and should exploit them for all they're worth.

Retirement. Now that you have a child, it can be easy to forget about saving for your golden years. Even though your day-to-day expenses are higher, it's actually more important than ever to continue setting money aside for retirement. That's why having access to a tax-advantaged retirement account such as a 401(k) is the biggest benefit of working. It allows you to contribute up to $16,500 a year in pretax dollars into an investment account. Your returns then grow tax-free until you take the money out upon retirement. (Watch out. Should you take it out sooner, you will be penalized.) Best of all, many companies also offer their employees a match, which means it will match your contribution up to a certain amount, say, 3 percent. That's free money that no parent should walk away from.

Taking advantage of a 401(k) is also a much better deal than what's offered to nonworking folks. As I mentioned earlier, a stay-at-home parent can set aside up to only $5,000 in a tax-advantaged spousal IRA account. On top of that, there are income restrictions for participation. Not so with a 401(k).

Health insurance. The only benefit that may rival a retirement plan is health insurance. Sixty percent of employers offer their workers a choice of plans. It's your job to figure out which one is best suited in terms of coverage and affordability for your growing family. One surprise for many couples is how much their premiums skyrocket once a new baby enters the picture. Although you may have been able to afford your firm's PPO before your daughter or son arrived, you may now need to rethink that plan and switch to the cheaper HMO option. (I'll talk more about saving money on health care in Chapter 7.)

In some cases, it may actually make more sense for you and your spouse to split your coverage between two corporate plans.

Why? Many companies charge different premiums depending on who's covered. Often, a family plan that includes both spouses and children costs considerably more than an individual plan or even an employee-and-children option that covers only one spouse and the kids.

Flexible spending account, health care expenses. If you thought there were a lot of prenatal visits, just wait until you see how often you take your little one to the pediatrician. To help cover these new medical costs, find out if your employer offers a flexible spending account (FSA) for health care expenses. In 2007, 73 percent of large firms (200 or more workers) and 20 percent of small companies (3–199 workers) offered one as a benefit, according to the Kaiser Family Foundation.

What is an FSA? It allows you to set aside pretax dollars for medical expenses that aren't reimbursed by your health insurance plan, including your family's deductible, copayments for pediatrician visits and prescriptions, and many uncovered expenses such as contact lenses and even infant Tylenol. For someone in the 33 percent federal tax bracket, that means saving about $400 on every $1,000 of medical bills when you factor in the Social Security and Medicare taxes you don't have to pay on deductible dollars.

Perhaps the most important thing to know about FSAs is that it's probably the only tax break you'll qualify for on health care expenses. That's because most young families don't have medical costs that exceed 7.5 percent of their adjusted gross income, the level where you can begin to itemize medical deductions on your income taxes. The one downside is that you need to accurately estimate how much to put into your FSA. Any money that goes unused in a given year is forfeited to your employer. So it's best to guess too low rather than too high. You can adjust your contribution to an FSA on an annual basis, based on your expenses of the past year and how you estimate they'll change for the next year.

I'll talk more about how to best exploit this gem in the health care section.

Health savings accounts. If your employer doesn't offer an FSA, it may provide its employees with access to a health savings account (HSA). HSAs are very similar to FSAs since they also allow you to set aside pretax dollars for health expenses. The main difference is that an HSA is for qualified high-deductible health plans, and any money that isn't used in a given year can be rolled over for future expenses. Also, the money in your HSA can often be invested.

Flexible spending account, child care expenses. If you're paying someone else to watch your kid, you won't want to miss out on the dependent care FSA. It allows you to set aside up to $5,000 in pretax dollars to help pay for child care that you need in order to work. To qualify, the person you've hired to watch your little one must have a tax identification number. So if you're paying your neighbor under the table, you won't be able to take advantage of this perk.

Another nice benefit of the dependent care spending account is that as your child enters school, you can still use pretax dollars to help pay for summer camp and after-school care up to age twelve.

Backup child care. While this perk is hardly universal, some companies offer their employees access to backup child care services. Typically, a firm will contract with a day care provider, such as Bright Horizons Family Solutions, which allows parents to drop off their young children for the day when school is closed or a nanny gets sick. Employers may also offer to pick up the cost for a babysitter up to a certain number of days per year. This perk can help parents go to work and save them hundreds of dollars a year.

Flexible spending account, commuting costs. Unless you work from home, it's going to cost you to get to the office. If you're lucky, you may be able to get a small discount on your commuting costs. While this isn't a direct child-related benefit, parents should take advantage of commuter programs since the extra cash will help pay for costly kid expenses, including child care.

The IRS allows workers to set aside pretax dollars for van pools and mass transit ($230 a month) or qualified parking ($230 a month), which includes parking where you take mass transit or the location where you pick up the van pool. Unfortunately, the actual cost of driving itself doesn't qualify since fuel, maintenance and auto insurance costs are not covered.

In the next chapter I'll help you find more ways to stretch your paycheck by walking you through all the various tax breaks that Uncle Sam offers to families.

CHAPTER 4

WHO SAYS UNCLE SAM DOESN'T CARE?

Common Misconception:
Children make a great tax write-off.

The Reality:
The IRS does allow plenty of tax breaks for dependents, but Uncle Sam doesn't always make it easy to claim them.

The Bottom Line:
Even if you use an accountant, it's important for you to figure out which deductions and credits your kids may qualify you for.

One of the first lessons parents learn is that children are expensive. Between baby gear, child care costs and college tuition, it's a wonder anyone can afford to keep having babies. Fortunately, Uncle Sam offers some attractive tax breaks to help families foot the bills.

The good news is that most families will qualify for a handful of tax breaks. The bad news is that the most generous ones come with income limitations. Child-related tax credits, in particular, are geared toward middle- and lower-income families. This chapter will summarize all of the available child-related

THREE STEPS FOR TAX SAVINGS

Follow the road map below so that you don't overlook any valuable tax-saving possibilities. Remember, if you don't claim them, the IRS won't voluntarily give them to you.

Step 1: Revisit Your Past

Take a few minutes to write down any life changes (such as the birth of a child) that occurred over the past tax year. Take this list and match it up against the various family-friendly tax breaks discussed in this chapter. If you use an accountant, make sure to give her a copy; it will help her think of the right questions to ask you come tax time.

Step 2: Review Your Options

Simply listing a child on your return doesn't mean Uncle Sam knows which tax breaks you should get. It's up to you to do the research and claim each deduction or credit you qualify for. To help you get started, this chapter summarizes the tax breaks you'll want to consider.

Step 3: Do the Math

Sometimes it's better to choose a company-sponsored benefit such as a medical flexible spending account over a deduction. Just remember, you can't get a tax break on the same expense twice, so you'll need to do the math to figure out which one is most advantageous for your situation. (See page 46 for more on how to crunch the numbers.)

tax deductions and credits, explain how much they're worth, and help you figure out which ones you qualify for.

I'll also help divorced parents figure out who gets to claim the kids on his or her return. As obvious as it may seem that running two households costs twice as much, the IRS isn't going to let both Mom and Dad take a personal exemption for their shared child.

It's a good idea to familiarize yourself with all of the available tax opportunities even if you use an accountant. That's because while a tax preparer should know to claim some of these—think dependent exemption—she may not know that you send your toddler to day care and would then qualify for a child and dependent care credit. Qualify for even a few family-friendly tax breaks and you could save thousands of dollars each year. That buys a lot of baby formula and soccer cleats.

GETTING STARTED

The birth of a child is a classic example of the kind of event that can affect your taxes. As Jennifer Share, the accountant and mother of four whom you met in Chapter 1, says, "I wouldn't have another child just to get an extra deduction, but the write-offs do help." Jen even wished her second child, who was due in January, would come a bit early to give her and her husband an extra year of child-related savings. As luck would have it, her son arrived on December 20 and the Shares got to claim an additional dependent exemption for that entire year.

Having another child isn't the only way to get a tax break, though. As you prepare your return each year, take a good look at any other major life changes over the past twelve months. Did a stay-at-home parent go back to work and now the kids are in day care? Or, if you have a special-needs child, did he start attending a private school? As you tally any adjustments, you'll be better able to identify which tax benefits may apply to you.

Again, this exercise is useful even if you work with an accountant. People often meet with their

TAX TIP

Everyone needs a Social Security number, even an infant. You can't claim your child on your return if he doesn't have one. Most hospitals provide new parents with the necessary forms, but don't worry if the paperwork somehow got overlooked. You can directly contact the Social Security Administration at any time for an application at SocialSecurity.gov.

FILING A TAX RETURN FOR YOUR CHILD

A dependent child with investment income over $950 or earned income over $5,700 needs to file a 1040. Since your little ones are clearly too young to fill out the paperwork on their own, you'll have to do it for them. If the earnings are only from interest and dividends, including capital gains distributions, and are less than $9,500, the government will allow you to include your child's income on your tax return. Although it may seem easier at the time, it could end up costing you if that money pushes your total income higher and you no longer qualify for valuable tax breaks.

tax preparers just once a year, so your accountant simply may not know you and your family well enough to anticipate all the tax breaks you could qualify for, says Mark Nash, the author of *PricewaterhouseCoopers 2009 Guide to Tax and Financial Planning.* The more homework a client can do before a meeting, the more informed your accountant will be and the more complete your tax return.

TAXES 101

Here's a rundown of all of the child-related tax saving opportunities you may qualify for. Understand that there are two types of tax breaks: deductions and credits. Don't confuse them. Deductions are subtracted from your gross income and lower your taxable income. Credits are far more valuable since they allow you to subtract dollar for dollar the amount you owe on your tax bill, or add the amount to your refund.

FOR ANYONE WITH KIDS

Deductions

Dependent exemption. Every member of your household potentially counts toward a tax-deductible exemption on the family tax return. During the 2009 tax year, each exemption can mean up to a $3,650 deduction. So if you're married with two kids, your family could qualify for four exemptions worth a $14,600 tax deduction.

DIVORCE AND YOUR TAXES

 As if getting divorced wasn't hard enough, things can get even more complicated when you try to figure out which parent gets what tax break.

Let's start at the beginning and keep things simple. As a general rule, the custodial parent, or the one who takes care of the children for more than 50 percent of the time, gets to claim the kids as dependents and is entitled to all of the deductions and credits.

There is a special rule, however, that allows a custodial parent to release his or her right to claim the children to the other parent. (Go to the IRS Web site, irs.gov, for more on this.) The noncustodial parents cannot, however, claim the coveted head-of-household status, since the children don't live with them for the majority of the year.

Things get a bit trickier when parents share custody. Ideally, your lawyers have worked out who gets what and made sure that everything is spelled out in the divorce agreement. If not, the IRS generally favors the parent with the higher adjusted gross income and lets him or her claim the child on his or her taxes.

Alimony. If you receive spousal support, remember to claim it as income on your return. In other words, make sure you don't spend all of it before the end of the year; you're going to owe taxes on it. Meanwhile, the parent who is making alimony payments gets to deduct the money on her taxes.

Child support. Unlike alimony, the parent receiving child support doesn't need to report the money as income and pay taxes on it. And the person paying the support also doesn't get to write it off.

&

Unfortunately, there are some income restrictions on this deduction. During 2009, the exemption starts to decrease once your adjusted gross income reaches a certain threshold and then disappears entirely once that income exceeds the following phase-out range:

Type of Return	Phase-out Range for Income
Married couples filing together	$250,200–$372,700
Married couples filing separately	$125,100–$186,350
Single/head of household	$208,500–$331,000

Looking ahead to the 2010 tax year, the IRS may start to get a bit more generous and slash the phase-out limits. So make sure to check with the IRS Web site (irs.gov) for any changes.

Credits

Child tax credit. In addition to the dependent exemption, the IRS also allows qualifying families to take a $1,000 tax credit for each child under seventeen. So if you have three kids, you can slash $3,000 off your tax bill. This credit has some income limitations, which vary based on how many children you have. So check with the IRS or your accountant to see how large your particular credit will be. In 2009, the child tax credit started to phase out when the following modified adjusted gross incomes were exceeded:

Type of Return	Income Threshold
Married couples filing together	$110,000
Married filing separately	$55,000
Single parents	$75,000

Earned income tax credit. Young parents who are just starting out in their careers should look into the earned income tax credit. It's geared toward helping families with lower incomes and can be worth as much as $3,043 for those with one child, $5,028 for parents with two children, and $5,657 for those with three or more kids. In 2009, to qualify, your adjusted gross income needed to be below the following thresholds:

FAMILIES WITH ONE CHILD	
Type of Return	**Income Threshold**
Married filing together	$40,463
Single parent	$35,463

FAMILIES WITH TWO KIDS	
Type of Return	**Income Threshold**
Married filing together	$45,295
Single parent	$40,295

FAMILIES WITH THREE OR MORE KIDS	
Type of Return	**Income Threshold**
Married filing together	$48,281
Single parent	$43,281

FOR PARENTS WHO ADOPT

Nearly 125,000 children are adopted by Americans each year. Ask any parent about the process and they'll tell you it's long and expensive. In fact, the average adoption costs $15,000, according to the Health Insurance Association of America, and international adoptions can easily exceed $25,000. Fortunately, there is a tax credit that can help ease the financial burden.

Adoption credit. The IRS allows new parents an adoption credit worth up to $12,150. Parents adopting a child with special needs can take the full credit even if their expenses total less than the value of the credit. (A qualifying special-needs

THE KIDDIE TAX

Parents used to be able to save on taxes by gifting their child's cash into a custodial account and then investing the money on their behalf. Once a son or daughter turned eighteen, all the proceeds in the account were taxed at the child's lower tax rate. But in 2008, the IRS made a change. Now, full-time students under the age of twenty-four who have unearned income above $1,900 are taxed at their parents' higher tax rate. The only way to avoid paying the kiddie tax is if the child's earned income exceeds 50 percent of the support he receives from his parents.

child is a U.S. citizen or resident whom a state determines cannot or should not live with his own parents and probably won't be adopted unless special assistance is provided.)

Generally, couples must file a joint tax return to qualify for the credit. And once again, there are some income restrictions attached. In 2009, the credit started to phase out when your modified adjusted gross income exceeded $182,180. It phased out entirely when your adjusted gross income exceeded $222,180.

FOR PARENTS WHO PAY FOR CHILD CARE

Credit

Child and dependent care credit. Two-income families with any children under thirteen years old qualify for a dependent-care credit to help cover child care expenses, as mentioned previously on page 46. In addition to day care and other traditional forms of child care, summer day camp also counts.

Although this credit is meant for working parents, the IRS also allows those looking for work, students and disabled moms and dads to claim it. The credit itself is worth 20 percent to 35 percent of child care expenses up to $3,000 for one kid and $6,000 for two or more children. That comes out to a reduction on your tax bill worth up to $1,050 for one child and $2,100 for two or more children. But be aware that there are income thresholds, as usual. For households with an income over $43,000, the credit shrank to just $600 for one kid and $1,200 for two or more children in 2009.

FOR PARENTS WITH SIGNIFICANT MEDICAL EXPENSES

Deduction

Medical expenses deduction. In a year when your family's medical bills are particularly high, you may be able to deduct a portion of your costs. The IRS allows taxpayers to write off medical expenses that exceed 7.5 percent of their adjusted gross income. Check with the IRS Web site for a complete list of all qualifying expenses.

FOR EDUCATION COSTS

Deduction

Saving for college. Depending on where you live, you may be able to deduct contributions to certain types of college savings accounts, such as a 529 plan. In New York, for example, residents are allowed to deduct up to $5,000 a year or $10,000 for married couples. I'll talk more about these plans and other ways to save for college in Chapter 8.

Credit

Lifetime Learning credit. The government wants to help you stay on top of your game. That's why the Lifetime Learning credit helps ease the financial burden of taking classes to improve one's job skills. While it's often used by parents who pay tuition for a dependent in college, Mom and Dad can claim it for their own studies, too. This could be especially useful for a stay-at-home parent who goes back to school to keep his professional skills up to date. So how much is it worth? You can claim a credit worth 20 percent of tuition and other expenses totaling $10,000, for a maximum of $2,000. The one caveat is that the Lifetime Learning credit can be used for only one family member in any given year.

In 2009, the income restrictions for the Lifetime Learning credit started to phase out at the adjusted gross incomes listed below.

Type of Return	Phase-out Range for Income
Married filing together	$100,000–$120,000
Single parents	$50,000–$60,000

For Indirectly Kid-Related Breaks

Selling a home. Nothing makes you yearn for a new, bigger home quite like the arrival of a baby. If you do plan on moving and need to sell your existing home first, the IRS lets married couples exclude $500,000 ($250,000 for single parents) in capital gains on the sale from their taxes. The one stipulation is that you need to have lived in your house for two of the past five years.

Haven't owned your home quite that long? Uncle Sam realizes that life can be full of surprises. That's why there is a tax law for "unforeseen circumstances" that lets you prorate the exclusion amount if you're forced to sell before the two years is up. And according to the IRS, having twins (or triplets or more babies from one pregnancy) is considered an unforeseen circumstance.

Credit

First-time home buyers. If you bought a house between January 1, 2009, and December 1, 2009, the government is giving you a one-time tax credit worth $8,000. (This is a gift from Uncle Sam. But if you move within three years, you'll have to pay it back.) This credit phases out for married couples with adjusted gross incomes that exceed $150,000 and $75,000 for single parents. "This is a way to help first-time home owners come up with the down payment and closing costs, which can keep young families from purchasing homes," says Dan Thomas, a CPA in Newport Beach, California.

Deduction

Donations. Donate clothing your son has outgrown and toys he no longer plays with and not only will you feel good about cleaning out your closets, you can write it off on your taxes. Just make sure to keep a list of every stroller or pair of pajamas you give away and estimate what the IRS calls its "fair market value," or the amount it would sell for on the open market. (You can find a list of suggested values on the Salvation Army's Web site.) Note that donations of stained onesies and other well-worn items don't count toward your tax write-off; Uncle Sam demands that everything be in "good used condition or better."

WHICH TAX BREAK SHOULD YOU CHOOSE?

Uncle Sam won't let you deduct the same expenses twice, and in some cases, it's more beneficial to choose employer-sponsored benefits over tax credits or deductions. It's up to you to figure out what is the most advantageous for your family's situation, but there are a few general guidelines.

Let's start with child care expenses. If you're lucky enough to have access to a flexible spending account at work, you should use it. In most cases, parents are better off choosing the FSA, says Dan Thomas. That's because the savings from using pretax dollars usually adds up to more than the child and dependent care credit. The average parent who has at least $5,000 in child care expenses could save as much as $2,000 versus just $600 (for one kid) or $1,200 (for two or more children) with the credit if his or her income exceeds $43,000 a year. If, however, your child care expenses exceed $5,000, you may be able to also claim the child and dependent care credit, as long as you don't claim the same expenses for both tax breaks.

Next, there are health care expenses. Once again, families with access to a flexible spending account should use it. An FSA allows employees to use pretax dollars to pay for up to $5,000 in medical expenses. That could be worth up to $2,000. The health care deduction, on the other hand, kicks in only for expenses that exceed 7.5 percent of your adjusted gross income. That's a pretty high threshold for most young families.

Finally, there's a tax choice to make for adoptive parents. If your employer offers you assistance with your adoption-related expenses, you should take the help. Any additional costs that aren't reimbursed qualify for the government's tax credit. Since adoption is so expensive, many families will be able to take advantage of both forms of help, but you must not claim the tax credit for expenses your employer already paid you for.

If all of these family-friendly tax breaks seem overwhelming, reread this section. It's really quite manageable once you get a handle on it. Yes, there are a lot of income restrictions to consider and rules to sort through, but your reward for doing so is that it can save a bundle of money—which you can put toward other things for your bundle of joy.

CHAPTER 5

WHERE SHOULD YOU NEST?

> **Common Misconception:**
> If I move to the suburbs, I won't have to worry about money anymore.
>
> **The Reality:**
> Nothing is cut-and-dried. While some things, including food and entertainment, are generally cheaper in the suburbs, other costs, such as commuting, may be higher. If you aren't careful, you could still end up spending more than you'd like.
>
> **The Bottom Line:**
> Think through all of your choices—your happiness is as important as your budget.

Many parents agonize over where to raise their children: Is it best to stay in the city? Move to a bedroom community a short distance away? Or travel out to the exurbs, where the homes are larger and cheaper? Unfortunately, all three options have trade-offs.

The wisest way to make this decision is to consider it from a couple of different angles. First, there is the lifestyle component. Are you the type of parent who wants to walk hand in

THREE STEPS FOR DECIDING WHERE TO LIVE

Following the three steps below will help you make a decision that's right for your family in both the short and long terms. Remember, you need to balance your budget and your lifestyle. If you do ultimately decide to stay in an area that's a bit out of your financial comfort zone, you'll have to find a way to live within your means, even if that includes giving up an extra bedroom or lavish vacations.

Step 1:
Figure Out Where You Prefer to Live

Did you cherish your own suburban upbringing? Or did you long for the excitement of more urban locales even as a child? Do you want to live in a bedroom community that's close enough to a city so that you can easily expose your children to museums? Or would you rather live further out, where land is cheap and the backyards are expansive? These are the types of questions you should start asking yourself as you ponder where to raise your little ones. While finances are important to consider, families can probably make a number of different living situations work within their budget, provided they're willing to make some monetary sacrifices in other areas.

Step 2:
Add Up *All* of the Costs

If you decide some kind of move is right for you, it's time to crunch the numbers so you can budget appropriately. Moving to the suburbs isn't strictly about comparing home prices inside and outside city limits. People in the suburbs have all sorts of expenses that city folks may not incur. If you previously lived someplace with a good public transportation system and didn't need a car, you will now need to buy one (or two) and insure it. If you work in the city, you'll need to factor in higher commuting costs. If the close-in suburbs within a short commute to the city don't save you enough money, you may want to consider moving further out, where the overall cost of living is cheaper.

Step 3: Hidden Considerations

As with so many decisions we make in life, moving from the city to the suburbs or from the suburbs to the exurbs could have some hidden trade-offs that you don't realize, including the need to sneak out of the office earlier than you really should to make that longer commute and still kiss the kids good night.

❧

hand with your child down a bustling city street while grocery shopping? Or do you prefer the quiet pace of the suburbs and having a backyard where your kids can run around?

Second, there are the finances. Urban living is expensive, especially if you reside in a less-than-ideal school district and decide to shell out thousands of dollars for private school. In that case, moving to the suburbs and sending your kids to public school could save you a bundle. But some of that "found" money will now need to go to other expenses, including the upkeep on two cars and a house. Once they factor everything in, some parents may discover they need to move further out from the city to an exurb to realize significant cost savings.

While parents can't ignore the reality of their budgets, they also shouldn't ignore their own happiness. If you move out to the suburbs from the city and find the change in lifestyle doesn't suit your family, you may decide to pack up your things and move back to where you started—and that's the most expensive decision, since you'll have to pay to move twice.

WHAT DO YOU REALLY WANT?

Before you call the movers, seriously consider where you and your family are going to be happiest. Do you see yourselves with a living arrangement more like that of the Huxtables from *The Cosby Show* or the Bradys from *The Brady Bunch*? As much as this book is about finances, you can't live your life strictly by your pocketbook, especially if certain money-saving decisions will lead you to resent your children because they were the reason you moved to a place that grates on your nerves.

In this section, I'll outline the advantages and disadvantages of living in the city, suburbs and exurbs. While your own parents and friends may try to sway you one way or another, each family needs to do what's right for them. And the sooner you identify what's right for you, the faster you can adjust your finances to make your situation work.

City Living

Many urban families have a tough time imagining themselves living anywhere but in a big city. Take Kristine Suzuki and Alex Sasieta, who live a mile from Lake Michigan in Chicago and love raising their toddler in such a vibrant place. "We like the energy and the cultural diversity," says Kristine. Although the couple own a car—which is useful for Costco trips—they prefer to walk most everywhere they go, from bookstores and restaurants to parks. Best of all, these city parents say they get to spend more time with their daughter since they aren't wasting one to two hours a day commuting to their respective offices.

Like many city parents, Kristine and Alex are a bit concerned about the quality of Chicago's public schools. Their hope is to send their daughter to the local magnet school, but they also realize that it may not live up to their expectations. If that happens, they're prepared to make the budgeting trade-offs required to write checks for private school.

Advantages

Pedestrian lifestyle. Families are within walking distance to shopping, entertainment, and restaurants, which is guaranteed to reduce the number of times you hear the dreaded phrase "Are we there yet?" More walking also promotes better overall health and fitness.

Culture. It's a heck of a lot easier to introduce your kids to art and music when museums and concert halls are in your backyard.

More stuff for kids. There's more to childhood than just soccer games. It may be easier for urban parents to sign their little ones up for foreign-language classes, museum programs and readings by famous children's authors. And don't forget about the zoos, aquariums and botanical gardens.

It's a melting pot. You don't need to hop on a plane to teach your kids about different cultures when your neighbors speak many different languages and came from locales all across the globe.

Convenience. Live in a dense city such as New York and there's no shortage of services that will deliver everything from groceries and diapers to dry cleaning and dinner to your front door.

Nightlife. When date night comes around, you'll have more options for letting off some steam and feeling like grown-ups again.

Public transportation. When your kids are teenagers you're freed from shuttling them back and forth to friends' houses, since they can then take public transportation on their own.

Disadvantages

It's pricey. At the risk of stating the obvious, urban living is more expensive than residing in the suburbs and exurbs. You'll pay more for everything from housing and lightbulbs to baby formula and preschool. This may leave families with less cash for vacations, baby-related activities or electronic toys for the adults.

Crime. Violent crimes are higher in most cities than the suburbs. So you'll need to watch your back and lock your doors.

Schools. While every city has a few standout public schools, the majority of them can't compare to the free education your kids could get in the suburbs. This leaves many urban parents with the headache of trying to navigate all the red tape of their city's public school system to find the right program. Or they're left to deal with the competitive process of applying to expensive private schools.

Space. Urban children are far more likely to bunk with a sibling or live in a room the size of a closet. And with no extra space for a playroom, walking in the living room is more likely to feature parental collisions with the latest plastic acquisition from Fisher-Price. No backyard, either!

More supervision required. City streets are no place for young children to roam on their own.

SUBURBAN LIVING

Many suburban families just don't understand why parents would raise their children anywhere else. As Lisa Green, a financial advisor who resides in Bryn Mawr, Pennsylvania, explains it: "I grew up in the suburbs and can't imagine living without trees and grass. The fact that the suburbs are cheaper than the city doesn't hurt, either." Before Lisa had kids, she lived in Philadelphia. When she and her husband began thinking about starting a family, they figured out that their mortgage payment on a four-bedroom house in Bryn Mawr was the same as their rent on a one-bedroom apartment and two parking spots in the city. But most appealing of all about Bryn Mawr is the fact that Lisa can just open her back door and let the kids play safely in the backyard while she's cooking dinner. "I feel like living in the suburbs gives the kids more autonomy since I don't have to watch them all the time."

Lisa says she doesn't miss living in Philadelphia since she's just a forty-five-minute drive away and can easily access restaurants and museums. A long commute isn't an issue, because Lisa works part-time, with many of those hours at home, and her husband works out of a home office. If they both had to drive into Philly every day and didn't get to see their kids as much as a result, she admits, they might reconsider their choice.

Advantages

More house for your money. For the same mortgage payment, a two- or three-bedroom apartment in the city can often be swapped for a four- or five-bedroom house in the suburbs, complete with backyard and free parking.

A no-hassle education. Choose an area with good schools and you won't have to worry about your child's education. Best of all, there are no stressful admission tests for the little ones.

Green space. No need to chaperone your kids at the local playground. Just open the back door and they can kick around a soccer ball in the yard.

Less crime. The suburbs may not be as safe as they once were, but most families still feel more secure outside of the city.

Disadvantages

Car culture. If you don't love driving, the suburbs may not be for you. Parents spend a lot of time behind the wheel, shuttling their kids back and forth to different activities. Not to mention the endless phone calls negotiating the car pool.

The commute. Unless you work in the suburbs, too, you're going to start spending a lot more time getting to and from the office. That's time you could have spent reading with your kids. And money you're spending on gas!

Fewer cultural activities. Smaller towns and cities often don't have the resources for their own art museums and concert halls. If they do have them, they certainly aren't on the same scale as what you'd find in the city.

Less to do. Dinner and a movie is a big night out in the suburbs. If you want something a bit more out of the ordinary, you may need to drive into the city, adding another hour or two to your babysitting bill.

Exurb Living

Lucy Ritter couldn't wait to move out of her townhouse in Manassas, Virginia (a suburb in Prince William County). "I wanted a larger home and my husband wanted more yard," she says. "We couldn't afford it in Manassas, so we moved out to Loudon County, where there's more space and the homes are cheaper." For the Ritters, that four-bedroom house on a third of an acre was worth moving further away from Washington, D.C., to a town called Ashburn that until relatively recently had been farmland.

Soon after moving in, the Ritters fell head over heels for their new community. In addition to the great schools and quieter streets, she also found she had something in common with most of her neighbors. "We were all around the same age and probably made around the same amount of money since these homes were what we could all afford." The Ritters quickly became fast friends with the other families on their

WHAT HAPPENS WHEN LITTLE EMILY GETS A FEVER?

It can be tough on families with small children when both parents commute long distances for work. If your child gets a fever or takes a bad fall, Mom or Dad could get an urgent phone call and need to rush home to pick the child up.

Here's another consideration: if you work in an office where "face time" is valued and leaving at 5:00 p.m. is frowned upon, taking on a long commute could force you to decide between kissing your son good night and missing out on potential promotions.

For this and other logistical nightmares, it's not uncommon for one parent to decide to take a job closer to home (or to quit altogether). While finding a new position may seem like an easy solution, it could affect the family's income because folks working in the suburbs typically get paid less than those in the city. So make sure you think this through and research salaries closer to your new home just in case one of you needs to change jobs. The last thing you want to do is buy a home that you can't afford if one parent needs to take a salary cut.

block and watched as their children grew up together playing in the cul-de-sac.

Advantages

Even more space for the money. That's right—the further you move from the city, the cheaper housing gets.

The great outdoors. Okay, you're not exactly living in the country, but you're a lot closer to it than city or suburban dwellers. The Ritters can get to the Potomac River for fishing and canoeing and to plenty of outdoor activities in West Virginia in about half an hour.

Newer housing. The exurbs are sprinkled with new developments, so the housing stock is relatively new and the homes have modern amenities young families want, including great rooms, media rooms and open kitchens.

People like you. Young families with similar means and values flock to the exurbs. This can make socializing easier when neighbors have much more in common.

Disadvantages

Less established communities. If you're looking for historic architecture and a sense of history, you're less likely to find it here. You're also less likely to stumble upon a quaint downtown. Instead, some developers are building strip malls into housing developments, complete with a Starbucks, to create a feeling of community.

More drive time. The definition of an exurb is a community that lacks a commercial center, so it's likely you'll be farther from work and have a much longer commute, especially if you work in the city. One way to fix this could be to negotiate the ability to telecommute a couple of days a week.

Limited public transportation. Say "public transportation" in the exurbs and your only option may be a commuter bus that leaves once an hour. And that's if you're lucky. Many other commuters may have to drive to a nearby suburb and fight with the locals for parking to pick up a train.

Far from culture. Be realistic. You're not going to drag your kids into the city to see a play or stroll through a museum on a whim. Outings will take more planning and may become less frequent.

Ruby Tuesdays rule. Don't expect a vast assortment of individual boutiques and unique restaurants. You're more likely to find big-box stores and chain restaurants in the exurbs.

LOCATION, LOCATION, LOCATION

 If you don't want to change your lifestyle but are thinking about moving because of the finances, relocating to a different part of the country could be a better solution for your family.

As Mona and Michael Berman planned to start their family, they decided to move from Washington, D.C., to Philadelphia. While they don't live in Center City (they reside in the Chestnut Hill area), they are still within the Philadelphia city limits—and remain urbanites. They were also able to trade their three-bedroom apartment for a five-bedroom house that's just a thirty-minute train ride to downtown Philly. When they want to walk, they stroll down Chestnut Hill's charming main street filled with restaurants and boutiques. "We moved here because there's no reason to work and strive so hard and barely get by in cities like New York or D.C. when we can live easily in Philadelphia."

To get an idea of your general cost of living in your city compared with other areas, check out Sperling's BestPlaces at BestPlaces.net.

Your neighbors' rules. Many new exurban areas are master-planned communities that come with a homeowners' association. What does this mean to you? The house may be yours, but the color you paint it or the length of your grass could be up to a committee.

DOING THE MATH

Once you've decided which type of setting appeals to you most as a parent, it's time to home in on what you can afford. The only way to do that is to look at what you're spending today and how that will change if you move. (Don't forget to include all those new expenses that come with having a baby.)

The mistake many families make is to simply compare home prices in one area versus another. This isn't an accurate comparison since there are so many other non-real-estate expenses associated with living in a city, suburb or exurb.

Here are some expenses broken down by neighborhood type that you need to consider before you make a down payment on a new home.

URBAN LIVING IS PRICEY

Hands down, you'll spend the most living in the city. Families can easily spend a million dollars on a two-bedroom condo in cities such as New York, Los Angeles and San Francisco. But real estate isn't the only expense urbanites face. Here's what else you'll have to watch out for.

The necessities. A simple trip to the grocery store will set you back a lot further in a city than in the suburbs. In places such as New York, everyday items including milk and diapers are at least 10 percent more expensive than in the surrounding suburbs. One way to save some money is to shop online at sites like Amazon.com and look for free-shipping specials.

Schools. According to the EPE Research Center, concerns about public schools in the city are well founded; there are thirteen urban school districts with graduation rates between 40 percent and 50 percent, including Dallas, New York City and Miami. Opt for a private school instead and you're on the hook for an average of $18,000 a year per child.

The tax man. All those police officers, sanitation workers and transit employees cost a lot of money and you'll be taxed quite a bit to support them.

CITY SAVINGS

Urban living isn't all about emptying your pocket. Here are a few places where you can actually save money in the city.

Commute. Walk to work and your commute is free. Or take public transportation and the round trip could cost you less than $5.

Car. In many cities families can get away with either having no car or, as in Kristine Suzuki's case, with having only one. In fact, the Suzukis drive their shared car so little that they spend less on auto insurance than their suburban counterparts, since they qualify for a low-mileage insurance plan.

Utilities. If you live in a 1,300-square-foot condo, it's going to cost a heck of a lot less to heat and cool it than that 3,500-square-foot house in the suburbs.

SUBURBAN LIVING AND ITS TRAPPINGS

The move from an apartment to a house can be a big financial shock for urbanites. Indeed, it can cost a lot more to maintain that home than city dwellers realize. Add those costs on top of the commute, and that cheap house may not be quite as inexpensive anymore—which may convince some that they need to move a bit further out to see the budget savings they were hoping for.

It's also possible that some parents who prefer urban life may find that the savings associated with the suburbs aren't large enough to justify the lifestyle change. If they learn how to work the city's public school system and have the kids bunk together, they might as well stay in their urban jungles.

Here are some additional items suburban families need to budget for.

The two-car family. It's hard to survive in the suburbs without the requisite two cars. Buy a relatively cheap Honda Accord, and after a down payment of $2,000, you're still on the hook for monthly car payments of at least $470 a month. Then add insurance. According to the Progressive Group of Insurance Companies, the average cost to insure a car is $1,600 a year. All in, adding just one car could easily add $600 to your monthly expenses.

The dreaded commute. It may not only take you longer to get to work but also cost you more. Whether you take a commuter train or drive (think gas prices), you need to factor in your new costs.

The utilities. It's no small thing to heat and cool a home in the suburbs. You'll also pay more to keep your water running and lights on. So don't be surprised if you suddenly find yourself repeating the annoying question your parents asked you during childhood: "Do you have a boyfriend at the electric company?"

Lawn care. A perfectly manicured lawn takes work. If you don't have the time—or the desire—to do it on your own, you'll need to hire help. In northern New Jersey, for example, lawn care costs $30 a week from the end of April to the end of November. At the beginning of the season, you'll have to spend a couple of hundred dollars on general cleaning.

The garbage man. The biggest surprise for many urbanites is that you may need to pay to have your garbage hauled away. There are also fewer kids now than thirty years ago shoveling driveways in the winter, so once the novelty of clearing your own driveway passes, you may end up hiring someone to do that for you, too.

Home owner's insurance. The bigger the home, the more expensive it is to insure. After all, you've got a lot more stuff the insurance company will need to replace if disaster strikes.

SUBURBAN SAVINGS GALORE

Real estate. Cheaper homes are one of the main reasons families flock to the suburbs. Move out of the city and kids no longer have to share rooms. Parents also don't need to whisper after the kids go to bed since the bedrooms aren't ten feet from the living room anymore.

Cheaper child care. Day care centers and preschools get considerably cheaper once you leave the city. You will, however, probably pay about the same in the suburbs for a nanny, especially if she's commuting from an urban area.

Schools. They're free and for the most part pretty good. If you send your kids to private school, they may come at a slightly cheaper price than those in the city.

Taxes. A majority of suburbs have much lower taxes than the city. There are a few exceptions, though, so make sure you do your research and find out how much you'll have to spend.

Cost of living. As mentioned earlier, everything from groceries and toiletries to restaurants and entertainment are cheaper than in the city.

EXURB LIVING REQUIRES HEFTY COMMUTING COSTS

Overall, families will experience many of the same savings and expenses as those in the suburbs. But here's where you'll potentially see some differences.

Commute. The further you live from the city or commercial center, the longer you'll have to drive and the more you'll pay to feed your gas tank.

THE FINAL BUDGET BREAKERS

You're not done quite yet. After you've figured out the type of life you want and where you can afford to live it, you should now add in the one-time start-up expenses. While these costs probably won't affect the "where to live" decision, they're important since they will dictate how much cash you'll need for the move.

The move itself. If you already own a home and need to sell it, you'll end up handing over as much as 6 percent of your equity to a real estate agent. You could also spend up to a couple of thousand dollars hiring a real estate attorney or title company to help you close the sale on one house and buy another. Then there are all of the bank's closing costs on the new property, which will set you back about 2 percent of the home's purchase price. And when all the transactions are complete, you'll still need to hire a mover to haul your stuff out to the suburbs.

Furnishing. If you're moving from a two-bedroom apartment into a four-bedroom house, you'll suddenly have a lot more rooms that need furniture. Remember, you don't need to fill them all at once. And there's nothing wrong with shopping on Craigslist.

※

Maintenance. If you moved further out so you could buy an even larger home and even more land, it will cost more to heat and cool it and mow that lawn.

Association fees. If you move into a planned community, you may get hit up with homeowners' association fees that could run $600 a year or more.

EXURB SAVINGS

Price per square foot. Your money buys a lot more real estate the further you move from the city. In many areas of the country you can swap a humble starter home in the suburbs for a five-bedroom house in the exurbs.

Cost of living. You may be able to save even more on groceries, toiletries, restaurants and entertainment in the exurbs.

Once you factor in all the possible considerations, figuring out where to live may feel complicated. Use the information in this chapter to help shape your decision, but ultimately, you should go with your gut instinct and do what seems best for your family. If you do end up moving someplace new and find it doesn't feel right, remember that you can always move again. But trying to stick it out for a little while—especially if you made the change for financial reasons—can also give you the time you need to adjust to a neighborhood and make new friends.

PART TWO

NO ONE EVER SAID KIDS WERE CHEAP

CHAPTER 6

FINDING (AND PAYING FOR) MARY POPPINS

Common Misconception:

I don't need to worry about child care until after the baby is born.

The Reality:

You snooze, you lose. Wait until your leave is nearly over and you may miss out on the highest-quality and best-priced options.

The Bottom Line:

Start early. Mom may feel silly interviewing babysitters and touring day care centers when she's still wearing maternity clothes, but it will maximize your options and help the family adjust to the expense of child care.

What often causes working parents the most stress? It's not the long hours at the office or trying to balance attending school events with important meetings. For many mothers and fathers, it's finding affordable, reliable and loving child care.

In just the two short years that I've needed child care for my daughter, I've had my share of difficulties. My worst experience was with her first day care center, when at eighteen months, my little girl started at what I thought was a creative and loving facility. Instead, I quickly learned that it was packing in as many kids as it could fit into a room, breaking New York City's child care laws that specify the maximum number of children allowed in any given class for her age group. When I complained to the director, I received a "Dear Parent" letter that said my daughter was no longer welcome at the school, effective immediately. I was then left scrambling for a babysitter so I could go to work the following Monday.

My story may sound a bit extreme, but I would challenge you to find any working parent who doesn't have a child care war story worth sharing. Even the best babysitters occasionally have their own family issues that keep them at home—perhaps a sick child—and can leave you without coverage on a day when you simply can't work from home.

While no child care situation is perfect, every family can find the best solution for their needs and their budget, with full-time babysitters, au pairs and day care being the three most popular options. When you get it right, you'll be so thrilled to know that someone you trust is looking after your little one, leaving you the peace of mind to focus on your job. Despite my initial experience, my daughter is now thriving in a wonderful day care center that's within our budget, and I never have to worry about her safety.

TIME TO TALK DOLLARS

It's no secret that child care is expensive, but some care options are pricier than others, and costs will vary somewhat based upon where you live. For instance, while full-time babysitters are the most expensive option in New York City, in Iowa hiring a full-time caregiver to watch your child may be cheaper than sending your kid to a formal day care center.

In this chapter, I'll try to give you some price ranges for what you can expect for different types of care, but ultimately

THREE STEPS FOR FINDING THE RIGHT CHILD CARE SITUATION

The three steps below will help you navigate your child care choices so that you, too, will soon be feeling just as confident with your decision.

Step 1: Pricing Your Options

Research child care options and costs in your area. For example, while a full-time babysitter runs upward of $30,000 in New York City, a similar caregiver in Iowa can cost just over $20,000. Once you know the prices for the different options in your area, you can rule out care that's simply too expensive for your family.

Step 2: Finding the Right Fit

Figure out what type of care you're most comfortable with. Speak with friends who have children in child care situations and figure out what's most natural to your family. I'll help you make your decision by providing you with a list of pros and cons for the three most common care giving situations: babysitters, day care and au pairs.

Step 3: Making the Hire

Once you've made your decision, it's time to line up your child care. If you choose a babysitter, I'll explain why you should consider paying her on the books. If you prefer day care, I'll help you reduce your chances of picking a dud, as I initially did. And if you go with an au pair, I'll explain what to watch out for. I'll also provide you with some favorite interview questions from parents who have already been through the process.

you will need to do your own research to find out exactly how much your local options will set you back, while weighing the pros and cons of each. This breakdown will get you started with a general cost overview.

GETTING PERSONAL: THE BABYSITTER OPTION

Cost: $30,000 plus a year. Full-time babysitters tend to be most prevalent in urban areas and their surrounding suburbs. The average cost of a caregiver ranges from $10 to $15 an hour for one child, and increases by 15 percent to 20 percent when you add a sibling. (Don't be surprised if you spend more than $30,000 per year caring for one child.) Should you employ an agency to help you find the right caregiver, you can expect to pay a few more thousand dollars in placement fees, according to the International Nanny Association. However, if you have more than one child, a babysitter may start to look like a more affordable option, since day care, by comparison, generally charges twice as much for two siblings.

Hidden costs: $6,000 a year or more. Many families choose to provide a babysitter with a cell phone, a stipend toward transportation (many New Yorkers buy their caregivers a monthly train pass worth around $80), two weeks' paid vacation and a Christmas bonus worth two weeks of salary. Once your toddler starts preschool (which is often only a few hours per week), you may still have to pay the caregiver full-time to keep him or her (even for the hours your little darling spends in class). If you don't pay up, your babysitter may quit and find another family willing to pay her full-time wages.

Cheaper alternatives. Sharing a babysitter with another family might be an option. Or pay a stay-at-home mom to watch your child.

A CULTURAL EXCHANGE: THE AU PAIR

Cost: $18,000 plus. An alternative way to get one-on-one care is to hire an au pair, a young adult from another country who moves in with your family and cares for your children for one to two years. According to Cultural Care Au Pair, an agency that places au pairs, hosting one of their caregivers in your home will cost you nearly $18,000 a year ($340 a week). This price includes all the fees charged by the agency and a $195.75 (for 2009) weekly stipend that you pay directly to the au pair.

Hidden costs: minimum of $1,200, but could be considerably more. As with a nanny, you will likely end up providing your au pair with a cell phone. If you need her to drive your kids around town, you'll also need to add her name to your auto insurance (which could cost between $500 and $1,200 depending on where you live) and pay for gas. You may even end up buying an additional car to accommodate the extra driver in the household. And don't forget, it's your responsibility to provide room and board. The bigger her appetite, the more you'll pay!

Cheaper alternatives. If you live near a college, find a student whose schedule works with your child care needs and who is willing to watch your kids in exchange for room and board or invite Grandma to come live with you for free in exchange for child care or engage other family for help.

CARE WITH CLASS: DAY CARE FACILITIES

Cost: $4,000–$22,000 a year. According to the National Association of Child Care Resource and Referral Agencies, the average cost for an infant in full-time day care ranges from $4,388 to $14,647 a year, based on a 2007 survey. But don't be surprised if the centers near you are even higher, particularly in large urban areas. Unlike babysitters, where adding a child means you pay less per kid, with day care, adding a sibling means your costs almost double, as day care centers typically provide parents with only a small discount for multiple children. Quality facilities, however, double as all-day preschools and you won't have to pay extra for the educational component.

Hidden costs: $150–$2,000 plus. Most day care centers ask families to help supply your child's room with diapers and wipes every two weeks. You may also be asked to help provide snacks. And don't forget those teacher appreciation gifts at Christmas and the end of the school year.

The biggest hidden cost will vary depending upon how flexible your work schedule is. If you can't work from home, you'll have to pay someone to watch your child when he's sick or when the school is closed. My daughter's center, which runs on a school calendar, has several weeks off for vacation during the year. While we try to time our holidays around the center's breaks, I still end up paying a babysitter for at least a few weeks a year.

USING FLEXIBLE SPENDING ACCOUNTS TO EASE THE CHILD CARE BURDEN

Who says employers can't be family-friendly? As I mentioned in Chapter 2, the IRS allows parents to annually set aside up to $5,000 in pretax dollars in a company-sponsored flexible spending account to help ease the burden of child care. The money can go toward a qualifying babysitter (provided you're paying her on the books), day care or an au pair. (Your caregiver simply needs to provide you with a Social Security number or tax identification number.) You can even use the pretax dollars to pay for summer camp. The average family can save around $1,800 by taking advantage of a child care flex spending account, according to WageWorks, a San Mateo, California–based benefits administrator. Contact your company's human resources department for more information.

FIND THE RIGHT FIT FOR YOUR FAMILY

Now that you know which options fit your budget, here comes the hard part: you have to choose the type of care that best fits your family. In this next section I'll walk you through the pros and cons of babysitters, au pairs and day care to help you decide which one is best suited to your family's needs and your child's temperament. (After all, there's no point dreaming about day care if you can't reliably pick up your child by closing time or an au pair if you don't have a spare bedroom.) Before making this important decision, you should also speak with friends about their personal experiences with different types of child care.

Be warned: some types of child care are more popular in some areas than others, but that doesn't make one better than another. In my neighborhood, I've found day care has a bit of a stigma among nanny-centric families. I'm glad I ignored the critical comments hurled my way. My somewhat reserved two-year-old is now much more social thanks to all of her new friends in class. She can recite the days of the week, count to ten in Spanish and twenty in English and differentiate between a blue jay and a cardinal, all skills her wonderful teachers taught her at school. Do what's best for you and your child, not what your neighbors think is right. Here's some information on each type of care that will help you make that call.

BABYSITTERS

For some families, a full-time babysitter is considered the BMW of child care. The thinking is that if you can afford to, there's no reason why you wouldn't hire one. Ambre Proulx, a New York City–based mother who works in asset management, was won over by the personal attention a babysitter would be able to give her infant. She also liked that hiring a sitter gave her some added flexibility in case she got stuck at the office. The downside? Ambre feels she has little control over what her son does during the day. Her biggest pet peeve is that her babysitter spends time in playgroups with other caregivers who feed their charges junk food, and her child inevitably indulges as well.

Pros

- **Individual attention.** Your child doesn't need to compete with other kids for attention.

- **You set the schedule.** You decide when and where your child eats, sleeps and plays. (Although, there's no guarantee your caregiver will follow your directions.)

- **Convenience.** A sitter shows up at your door before work, so you don't have to worry about getting the kids ready for the day or transporting them to day care before you head to the office.

- **Economies of scale.** The cost for two or more kids isn't that much more than for just one.

- **Flexibility.** If you need to occasionally work late, most babysitters are willing to accommodate you. (You will, however, need to pay them overtime.)

Cons

- **The price.** A babysitter for just one child could cost more than $30,000 a year.

- **The paperwork.** To make your sitter situation legal you'll need to get an employer identification number (EIN), buy insurance, and start withholding taxes from your caregiver's paychecks. (See page 84 for more on how to put your babysitter on the books.)

- **There's no one watching your babysitter.** So unless you have a nanny-cam, you'll be in the dark about what really goes on during the day.

- **She's always there.** In fact, your sitter will end up spending more time in your home than you will during the week. This arrangement may make those parents who cherish their privacy a bit uncomfortable.

- **There's no educational component.** Unlike day care, you can't expect your caregiver to stay on top of your child's language development and motor skills. If you want certain skills enforced, you'll have to pay for additional classes.

- **Unpredictable availability.** If your babysitter's sick, you have to stay home from work if you don't have backup care available.

Au Pairs

Dorothea Schlosser, a former consultant, was drawn to the idea of hiring an au pair because she wanted her kids to learn German. The Basking Ridge, New Jersey, native, who was raised bilingual, hired a young woman from Germany and instructed her to speak only her mother tongue while caring for the children. The plan worked, and now both kids are fluent in two languages. Dorothea admits that the relatively cheaper price versus other options was an additional selling point.

The downside? Dorothea and her husband lost a bit of their privacy with the addition of a live-in family fräulein. They now joke that they need to be more careful about how they dress around the house.

Pros

- **Price.** An au pair is a much cheaper alternative to a babysitter. The price also doesn't increase when you have multiple children.

- **Convenience.** It's hard for an au pair to be late for work since she lives with you. She can also drop the kids off at school if you need to leave early for work.

- **Language skills.** The world's a competitive place. Give your little one an edge by teaching him or her a foreign language. There's no better way to do that than by hiring a full-time live-in teacher.

- **You can take an au pair on vacation.** If you want some downtime on your next trip, you can bring along your caregiver for no added fee beyond the cost of an airline ticket and hotel room. Rent a house and she can sleep in the spare room.

MAKING IT LEGAL

Anyone who pays a nanny or babysitter (someone other than a parent or his or her own child and who is eighteen or older) more than $1,700 a year needs to make the arrangement a legal one. While the process is complicated and time consuming, companies such as GTM Payroll Services (GTM.com) and PayCycle.com can help by managing all the paperwork and cutting the checks for you. GTM Payroll, for example, charges an initial $95 registration fee and then up to $60 a month to calculate and withhold the taxes, prepare and issue the checks, and file the state and IRS taxes.

Here's what you need to do to pay your caregiver on the books. For more help, consult an accountant or IRS Publication 926.

1. Make sure your caregiver can legally work here. Have her fill out Form I-9, Employment Eligibility Verification (available at uscis.gov), and Form W-4 (found on the IRS Web site), which provides you with her legal name, address and Social Security number. Keep copies of these completed documents on file.

2. Apply for an employer identification number through the IRS.

3. Research local requirements with your state employment office. Most states require household employers to pay unemployment taxes and, if mutually agreed upon by family and employee, state withholding taxes and carry workers' compensation insurance. You must also complete and file a New Hire Report with your state.

4. Calculate withholding taxes. Withhold 7.65 percent for Social Security tax and Medicare tax. Your babysitter may also ask you to withhold federal and state income taxes. Just in case your math skills are a bit rusty, you can find an online calculator on the GTM Payroll Services Web site or SmartMoney.com.

5. Distribute paychecks regularly. Some states may have specific guidelines on pay cycles.

6. Make quarterly federal and state tax payments. Families can expect to pay 9 percent to 13 percent of their nanny's gross pay toward taxes, according to Guy Maddalone, of GTM Payroll Services. You're required

to pay your share of Social Security tax and Medicare tax, as well as federal and state unemployment taxes. Consult IRS Publication 926 for more information.

7. Prepare all paperwork for year-end tax filing. Provide your caregiver and the Social Security Administration with W-2s, and file Schedule H (Form 1040), Household Employment Taxes, with your federal income tax return.

Why go through all this trouble? Even if you aren't worried about getting caught by Uncle Sam, there are other reasons to keep your sitter legit. First, by paying taxes, you can use your flexible spending account to help offset your expenses. Also, your family is protected should your babysitter hurt herself while she's working in your home (if your state requires workers' compensation coverage). Finally, it's good for the caregivers, too, since some of the taxes go toward their Social Security fund.

Cons

- **Loss of privacy.** An au pair lives with you and is supposed to be treated like a younger niece. So expect to eat all of your meals together.

- **They're young.** According to Cultural Care Au Pair, au pairs start as young as eighteen (and they can't be older than twenty-six). And they typically won't have as much child care experience as a full-time babysitter.

- **You need to be accommodating.** If you want your au pair to be happy—and who wouldn't?—you'll have to help her adjust to our culture as well as your family. So if she's a picky eater who doesn't like your American cooking, you need to bone up on your wiener schnitzel, pierogies, or pad thai quickly.

- **Limited hours.** Au pairs are restricted to working only forty-five hours a week, according to Cultural Care Au Pair. So if you work past 5:00 p.m., you may need to hire another babysitter. Also, if your caregiver watches your kids all week, you'll need to get a different sitter for weekend date nights with your spouse.

- **It's a limited engagement.** Au pairs can stay with your family for only two years. So if you find you like the au pair experience, your children may need to welcome several caregivers before they reach elementary school.

- **Don't expect an au pair to clean your house.** Unlike a babysitter, who may be willing to act as a part-time housekeeper while the kids are napping, au pairs only take care of the kids. (You can, however, ask her to cook for your children and clean up any mess the kids make on her watch.)

WHEN THINGS DON'T WORK OUT

Cultural Care Au Pair says it has an 80 percent success rate matching families with caregivers. But what happens when you fall into the other 20 percent and just can't get along with yours? A good agency will try to find you a new au pair who is already in the country and who is also looking for a new family to work for. If you decide to go through the selection process from the very beginning and choose someone who is still living in their home country, you could end up without child care for an extended period of time.

DAY CARE

It isn't difficult to find parents who proselytize about day care.

Indeed, Nancy Bisaha, a college professor living in Poughkeepsie, New York, has a long list of reasons she recommends day care to all of her friends. She feels the group setting helped socialize her daughter and taught her to negotiate with other kids from a very early age. The environment is structured with educational yet playful activities, and television watching isn't an option. When the inevitable parenting challenges crop up, Nancy likes that she can turn to the teachers for advice. But most of all, she feels confident she's leaving her little one in trustworthy hands since there are always multiple caregivers present.

The downside: Nancy and her husband dread flu season. When her daughter gets sick, she can't go to day care, and that means Nancy and her husband, David, have to juggle their work schedules so one parent can stay home. Still, all in all, day care is the best solution for Nancy's child care needs. This list of other pros and cons will help you weigh the options for yourself.

Pros

- **Oversight.** Formal day care centers need to be licensed and meet a certain set of criteria, including how many teachers are required to watch a specific number of children.

- **No management skills required.** The day care center takes care of all staffing issues, including training, background checks and payroll taxes.

- **School's in session.** Most day care centers provide a full curriculum ranging from music to language development. Even one-year-olds will come home with art projects.

- **A sense of community.** Even working long hours, you'll get to know lots of other families.

- **Other children.** Kids enjoy learning from each other. What better way for them to do that than to be with their peers all day long? Children in day care also learn to socialize with other kids at a younger age.

Cons

- **No flexibility.** Most day care centers will charge you fines if you're even just a few minutes late.

- **Welcome to the sick ward.** Colds spread faster than a California wildfire when kids hang out together all day long. While you may not mind having a child with the sniffles, your boss will; if your son or daughter is ill, you have to keep the child home and miss work.

- **There's no shortage of rules.** Indeed, you may be asked to sign a multiple-page "parent agreement" outlining a list of regulations ranging from the types of food you can pack for lunch (nuts tend to be forbidden) to behavior that can merit your child's dismissal.

- **Less individual attention.** If your infant's crying, there's no guarantee someone will be able to comfort him immediately.

- **The steep price for siblings.** Send two kids to day care and you'll pay nearly twice the price. Typically, only a small discount is granted to families with multiple children.

HIRING YOUR CAREGIVER

Now that you know what type of care you want, it's time to select the caregiver that's right for you. How do you do that? Keep in mind that the more time and effort you put into this process, the happier you and your child will be. Like anything else, there are some very good nannies, day care centers and au pairs, and there are also some that just don't quite measure up. Here's some advice for finding the right person to pamper your little prince or princess.

BABYSITTERS

The best sitters are often found through word of mouth, including friends and colleagues. Nanny agencies can also be quite helpful, although they're expensive, often charging 10 percent of a caregiver's salary, according to the International Nanny Association. You can also look for babysitters on Craigslist and SitterCity.com.

If you don't use an agency, make sure you conduct a full background check on a caregiver candidate. You can start the process yourself by asking the applicant to fill out a standard employment application, which you can find online. Next, ask for three professional and personal references. And if she isn't a citizen, ask about working papers.

QUESTIONS TO ASK DURING A BABYSITTER INTERVIEW

Experienced parents I've interviewed suggest asking a prospective sitter these questions:

1. How long have you worked as a sitter? Do you have other child care experience?
2. Why did you leave your last family? What qualities are you looking for in a family?
3. What were the ages of the children you cared for?
4. What were your previous responsibilities?
5. Is there anything that you won't do? (Examples: children's laundry, cooking dinner.)
6. Do you know first aid and CPR? If not, are you willing to take a class?
7. How would you handle a (fill in the blank) situation? (Come up with situations that are important to you. For example, a child bumping her head at the playground, or the sitter's kids are sick.)
8. What is your philosophy on television? Junk food? (Ask about anything that is important to you.)
9. What is your philosophy on discipline? Are you comfortable with following my rules if they differ from yours?
10. How would you envision a typical day? (If you have an infant, ask how that day might change as the child ages.)

Then you'll need to verify the information. The Fair Credit Reporting Act requires families to get babysitters to sign a release allowing them to conduct a formal background check. For around $100 you can hire an online background check service. Look for a site that provides a comprehensive search across multiple databases. Companies specifically geared toward vetting sitters tend to include all the bells and whistles parents look for—think criminal records and national sex offender database checks.

Au Pair

If you want an au pair, you need to use a licensed agency, which you can find online. Once you've filled out the appropriate paperwork, a placement counselor will send you profiles for a few candidates to consider. After you've found a good potential fit, you will have the opportunity to e-mail back and forth with her and conduct an interview over the phone. Once you're satisfied you've made the right choice, the agency will work with you to coordinate travel arrangements.

Day Care

Don't choose a day care facility based on appearances alone. Ask neighbors and your pediatrician for recommendations. Check online with your local government child care bureau to see which nearby options are licensed and if any of them have outstanding violations.

Also be sure to check online child care sites for comments from other parents. While the responses are sure to be mixed, you may notice a theme to some of the complaints. If you're concerned, ask the director about the posts.

Even after you've made your decision about what type of care you want and you've hired the caregiver, don't be surprised if you later feel you want a change. Unfortunately, it can sometimes take a few tries to find the right situation for your family. It's also true that as your child grows older, your needs may evolve. For example, a nanny who's great with infants may not provide your toddler with enough stimulation. It's always a good idea to reconsider your child care as your child reaches different stages and your family expands.

QUESTIONS TO ASK DURING AN AU PAIR INTERVIEW

Since an au pair's job is similar to a babysitter's, feel free to use many of the same interview questions. Here are some additional things you may also want to ask a candidate:

1. Have you been away from home before? For how long and where? Did you miss your family terribly?
2. Do you speak English? (Pay attention to this during the interview, since you need a caregiver who can communicate effectively in an emergency.)
3. Can you drive, and do you have a valid driver's license?
4. What experience do you have caring for children?
5. Do you have younger siblings you helped care for?
6. If I called (name of employer or family in babysitting), what do you think they would say about you?
7. Will you be comfortable living in my type of setting? (Mention whether you live in a city, suburb or small town.)
8. Are you willing to help out around the house? (Clean up after the kids, cook them lunch, etc.)
9. Are you comfortable living by our family's rules? (List things that are important to you, such as eating together as a family, coming home by a certain time in the evening, not having boyfriends sleep over, etc.)
10. Do you smoke?
11. What are your goals after your year here?
12. What are you hoping to get out of this experience?

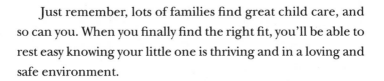

Just remember, lots of families find great child care, and so can you. When you finally find the right fit, you'll be able to rest easy knowing your little one is thriving and in a loving and safe environment.

DAY CARE QUESTIONS

Once you've found a few centers you like, schedule a tour of each. These questions for the day care center directors will help ensure that you're making the right choice. If they won't answer them or give you responses you don't like, move on to another facility.

1. What is the child-to-teacher ratio in *all* of your classrooms? (Remember, your child will move to different classes as she grows older.)
2. How much is tuition? Is there a waiting list?
3. What are the hours? What is the late policy?
4. What is the educational background and typical tenure for the care-givers?
5. Does the school have adequate indoor and outdoor play space?
6. What is the facility's philosophy on (fill in the blank) and how does it ensure that those beliefs are carried through in the classrooms? (Ask about what's important to you, including education, discipline, potty training, eating, etc.)
7. Can I bring my child in for a morning to see if he likes the program? (This may not be appropriate for infants, but it's a good exercise for one-year-olds and older children.)
8. Does the facility turn into a preschool as the children age? What is the curriculum?
9. Can I speak with other parents who have children attending the program?
10. What type of child tends not to thrive at your school?

CHAPTER 7

AVOIDING
A HEALTH
SCARE

Common Misconception:

It's not a big deal if my kids get sick. I'll just take them to the doctor and my insurance will cover it.

The Reality:

Your health insurance will cover only a portion of your growing family's care. While one appointment, copay or blood test for the kids might not feel expensive, it all adds up to some real money.

The Bottom Line:

When you have children, your health spending will go up. Try using doctors in your insurer's network and set aside as much as you can in a flexible spending account (or health savings account) to help pay for expenses that the health plan doesn't pick up.

Before you had children, you probably went to the doctor only on rare occasions. You didn't worry about budgeting for health care expenses. And news stories about the rising cost of health care were primarily the concerns of other folks.

Once kids enter the picture, that all changes. Children get sick. A lot. Their germs quickly spread around the household, infecting everyone. Trust me, I know. From my daughter I've caught everything from common colds to Coxsackie, a nasty virus that causes blisters on the hands, feet and throat. As useful as the Internet is for diagnosing mysterious ailments, it's no substitute for a real doctor's examination—and all of those office visits and lab tests can quickly add up.

This helps explain why your health insurance starts costing more once you add children to your plan. According to the Kaiser Family Foundation, a single person pays just $721 a year for employer-sponsored health coverage, while a family shells out $3,354.

At a time when health care costs are rising at 5 percent a year, parents can no longer be passive health care users. The good news is that if you manage your insurance and benefits properly, your health care shouldn't bleed you dry.

HEALTH INSURANCE 101

Tawnya Stone, whom you met in Chapter 2, took her health insurance for granted when she had her first child. She paid $15 a paycheck toward her premium and just $100 in out-of-pocket expenses for all the birth-related medical costs. "We didn't realize how good we had it," she says.

When the Stones had their second child, they suffered an acute case of sticker shock. Now that Tawnya was a stay-at-home mom, the family had to buy into her husband's employer's plan. Their premiums skyrocketed to $500 a paycheck (or $1,000 a month) and the couple got hit with $3,000 in

THREE STEPS TO MAXIMIZE YOUR HEALTH INSURANCE

Here's a breakdown of how you can take a proactive approach to your health and contain your family's medical expenses.

Step 1: Understand What You've Got

Most families get their health insurance through an employer's plan, which can vary widely. They also change from one year to another as employers tweak benefits while trying to save money, so it's important that you read your benefits booklet (also called a membership manual) and fully understand what medical care is covered and what's not under each available option. You also need to figure out how much you can expect to pay out of your own pocket for medical treatment. Check with your human resources department during your firm's annual open enrollment period to find out what changes were made to the plan from the previous year.

Step 2: Use Your Insurance Smartly

How much your family spends on health care will, in part, depend upon how effectively you utilize your plan. Now that you understand how your insurance works, it's a good idea to audit your medical usage and see where you could save money. If your child's pediatrician is out-of-network, can you find one you like who's in-network? You can also be strategic and try to schedule all of your expensive medical procedures for the same calendar year and take advantage of a deductible that's already been paid off.

Step 3: Use Pretax Dollars for Expenses

There is some good news on the health care front. As I mentioned in Chapter 3, if you have access to a flexible spending account (FSA) or health savings account (HSA), you can use pretax dollars to help pay for out-of-pocket expenses. I'll explain later how to best put these accounts to work. Even if you don't have an FSA or HSA, you may still be able to write off your medical expenses if they exceed 7.5 percent of your adjusted gross income.

out-of-pocket expenses for the birth. The Stones quickly learned that just because they were paying more for their insurance, they weren't getting better coverage—in fact, they were getting far less.

Before you're on the hook for thousands of dollars in out-of-pocket expenses, make sure you understand how your health insurance works and figure out how much protection it really offers you. This is especially important if you have a choice of plans through your employer or if you're buying coverage on the open market.

WHAT'S AVAILABLE

Most health plans are either a health maintenance organization (HMO) or a preferred provider organization (PPO). Here's how the different plans work.

HMOs

An HMO is typically a plan where you must select a primary care physician (PCP) who then acts as a gatekeeper for your medical care. If you have an ailment, whether it's chronic back pain or a scratched cornea, you must see your PCP, who then decides if she thinks you need a specialist. All doctors must also be in a carrier's network. (Some HMOs will allow you to see an out-of-network physician, but the deductible is so prohibitive that it will likely mean that you're paying for the entire visit out of your own pocket.)

If you go with a restrictive plan like this—and play by its rules—the upside is that you'll pay smaller premiums and lay out only a nominal copayment of about $25 for every office visit. The disadvantage is that you may not be able to see the pediatrician your best friend recommended to you. You may also find that it takes longer to get an appointment with a specialist since you first have to get a diagnosis from your primary care physician.

The bottom line: HMOs are affordable and a great option for young families that live in states such as Massachusetts and California, which have strong networks of doctors in most places. But they do have limitations, and you may need to think twice about choosing one if few doctors in your area accept your insurer's plan.

PPOs

PPOs offer families more flexibility, but they come with a cost. Members can see any doctor they want, whenever they want, without a referral from a primary care physician. As with an HMO, when you see an in-network doctor, you will pay only a nominal copayment. But if you choose to see an out-of-network provider, you're on the hook to pay first a deductible and then an average of 20 percent or 30 percent of the bill. This is called your coinsurance.

Making matters worse, when patients go out of network they no longer have an insurance company negotiating rates with doctors on their behalf. A doctor's full "retail price" could be as much as 50 percent more. And if the bill is above what the insurer deems "reasonable and customary," the patient gets stuck paying the difference. In an effort to save money on premiums, some employers will also trim the percentage of "reasonable and customary" they're willing to pay. While one employer may agree to pay 90 percent of "reasonable and customary," it could just as easily agree to pay only 80 percent. Guess who pays the difference? You.

The bottom line: Although PPOs come with higher premiums and larger out-of-pocket expenditures, some families will be better served by them. This is the case when a child or other family member has special medical needs and requires seeing specialists who aren't in an insurer's network. They're also the better choice if the HMO your employer offers doesn't have a robust network of physicians.

FLYING SOLO

When you have a family, you can't afford not to have health insurance. Even if you and your spouse tend to be relatively healthy, kids are always falling down and catching colds and other mysterious ailments that require medical attention. So if you're leaving a corporate job to start your own business or work for a small employer that doesn't offer health coverage, you'll need to buy an individual policy for you and your loved ones.

Getting Started

If you're used to corporate health plans, you may be incredulous when you see how much insurers charge individuals. That's because employers tend to subsidize insurance by paying more than half of a premium's full price. Large groups are also able to negotiate better rates. When you're on your own, expect higher monthly premiums, larger copayments, inflated deductibles and fewer benefits. And unlike employer-sponsored plans that have to accept everyone at the same rate, private plans in many states are underwritten based upon your age, health status and medical history. A preexisting condition such as asthma could cause an insurer to hike your premium or add a rider that excludes an ailment you need the insurance to cover. If this happens to you, shop around and you may find another company willing to cover your preexisting condition.

For better or for worse, insurance is regulated in every state. In some places, including New Jersey, New York and Vermont, insurers must accept every applicant. While this is good news for people with health problems, it also means that even young, healthy families will pay through the nose since everyone's premiums are high to help cover the sick. In other states, including California and Florida, there are fewer restrictions, so younger folks tend to pay less while older and less healthy people cough up more.

Buying It

Before you do anything else, see if you're eligible for COBRA. (COBRA is a federal law that requires certain employers to provide former employees with the option to purchase health insurance.) In most cases, it's smarter to sign up for your former employer's plan for the full eighteen months than to go out onto the open market. You will have to pay the full premium on your own, including the part your former employer used to pick up, but the coverage is typically more comprehensive and cheaper than comparable plans sold to individuals. (As mentioned in Chapter 1, you may be eligible for a nine month subsidy if you were laid off between September 1, 2008, and December 31, 2009.)

If keeping your previous insurance isn't an option, go to a Web site such as eHealthInsurance.com to get an idea of what prices are like in your area. Next, contact a seasoned local insurance broker to see if he or she can do any better than what you found online. Contact the National Association of Health Underwriters (nahu.org) for a listing of local brokers.

Finally, check to see if you can get coverage through a professional trade organization or small business association, since groups tend to get lower rates. Also, some states will allow small businesses with as few as two employees to qualify for small business rates.

If you're still having trouble finding an affordable policy, the easiest way to reduce your premium is to look for a high-deductible plan that comes with a health savings account (HSA). While families will have to front a deductible of at least $2,300, you could ease the burden by using pretax dollars in an HSA to fund it.

You can also check out CoverageForAll.org, a Web site that helps families see if they're eligible for free or low-priced health insurance in their state.

⊗

OTHER TYPES OF PLANS

Some companies also offer point-of-service (POS) plans (a hybrid between HMOs and PPOs) and exclusive provider organization (EPO) plans (which often don't allow members to see health care providers outside of the network). Since the benefits between plans can vary greatly, you'll need to go through the membership manual and see if it offers what your family needs.

READ THE FINE PRINT

Because employers have options when they select a health care plan—meaning they take away or add benefits to fit their budgets—it's especially important that you read through all the paperwork. When in doubt about whether a particular procedure or treatment is covered, call the customer service number and ask. But be aware that even calling isn't always foolproof.

When my daughter was a toddler, we were told she would benefit from speech therapy. As a dutiful health care consumer, I first called my insurer to see if it was covered, and was thrilled when I was told that it would be. But later when I submitted the claim, it got rejected. When I followed up, I was told the first representative must have misread my plan benefits. I was out a cool $500. The takeaway is you should always double-check the membership benefits booklet yourself to confirm that what customer service tells you matches your particular benefits plan.

STRATEGIZE

Once you have a handle on your plan, you can go through your family's habits and make sure you're best utilizing your insurance. Here are some questions to ask yourself.

- **Kids mean more doctors . . . am I staying in-network?** With the arrival of a new child you'll need to choose a pediatrician, and later a dentist and countless other medical practitioners. Are they and your own existing physicians in the plan's network? If not, consider finding ones who are. Since you're likely to have the same plan as your coworkers, you can start off by asking them for recommendations. If that doesn't work, go through the insurer's list to find a new doctor or dentist who's convenient to you. Chances are one of your other doctors may have a recommendation. When all else fails, consider trying new doctors until you find one you like. While this may take a while, you'll find a great one eventually and save a bundle paying only a copay.

- **Kids mean more prescriptions . . . am I overspending on medications?** A kiss and a Dora the Explorer bandage can't cure everything. One of the easiest ways to waste money is to overpay for your family's medications. In fact, spending on drugs makes up 43 percent of out-of-pocket expenditures, according to the Kaiser Family Foundation.

What can you do to lower your family's drug costs? The next time your child's pediatrician pulls out his prescription pad, ask about a generic medication. Nearly 75 percent of all FDA-approved drugs have generic counterparts, according to the Kaiser Family Foundation. The insurance copayment for no-name remedies is typically under $10. You could do even better if you shop around. Discount retailer Wal-Mart and warehouse store Sam's Club charge just $4 for up to a month's supply of more than four hundred generic drugs. Target offers similar pricing on three hundred generic medications. Also check with warehouse store Costco, which tends to charge 50 percent less than regular pharmacy chains for no-name medications, or try your local grocery-store pharmacy for deals.

If there is no generic version of the medication you need, ask your doctor if there's a remedy on your insurance company's preferred drug list. Most drug plans have something called a formulary, or list of medications they cover. For a generic drug you'll pay the smallest copayment, about $10. A preferred drug will come at a slightly higher cost, perhaps $25, but much less than one on the nonpreferred list, which is usually reserved for newer, more expensive drugs that could cost $35 or more. Often there are a handful of medications in the same class that provide similar therapeutic benefits, so ask your doctor if she has a true preference for which one you or your little ones take. Think of it as like seeing a doctor that's in-network versus one who's not.

Finally, if any of your family members take a medication regularly, consider ordering it by mail through your employer's

FIGHTING A CLAIM

If your health plan denies a claim, fight it. Here's how you can win the dispute.

Human Errors

The majority of claim denials are caused by simple human error. For example, if your doctor accidentally marks the wrong procedure code on a claim, it will get denied. The trouble is, when you receive your explanation of benefits (EOB) in the mail, there's no way to know what error was made. To clear up the confusion, you'll need to call a customer service representative, who can walk you through your claim and resubmit it once the two of you figure out what went wrong. For the quickest resolution, make sure you have all of your paperwork in front of you when you make the call, and keep meticulous records of your conversation.

Make Sure It's Covered

The second most common reason a claim gets denied is because a plan didn't cover a certain medical procedure or treatment in the first place. When this happens, there's nothing a customer service rep or regulator can do to help you.

Requesting a Formal Review

If your medical procedure or appointment is covered and you strike out with customer service, you have the right to request a formal review with your insurer. This can be as simple as writing your health plan provider a letter and supplying copies of your paperwork. Just make sure you don't procrastinate too long; most health plans will give you only a limited amount of time to file your grievance, usually about sixty days.

Regulators

Fighting a claim can be about as much fun as trying to reason with a two-year-old. Still, resist the temptation to give up if you get nowhere with your insurer. If your health plan says it won't pay for a treatment because it's "not medically necessary," you have the right to a review by an outside panel of doctors. Contact your state department of insurance and file a complaint.

You can even do this quickly online. What are your chances of reversing an insurer's decision? Pretty high. Decisions are reversed about half of the time when they're reviewed by state regulators, according to the Kaiser Family Foundation.

Self-Funded Plans

If you work for a large employer with a self-funded health plan (this is when your company pays its own claims but uses an insurer as an administrator), you'll need to file your complaint with the federal government through the Department of Labor's Pension and Welfare Benefits Administration. Your chances of getting a denial reversed are a bit lower with self-funded plans, unless a benefits advisor can prove that your employer administered your plan unfairly or if decisions weren't made uniformly for all of the plan's members. Your best bet is to get a health care advocate on your side, who knows how to communicate effectively with health plans. Your state department of insurance or state attorney general's office can help you find a trusted advocate in your area. While he or she can't force your health plan to change its mind, advocates understand how the plans work and can ask the right questions to get you the medical care you need.

pharmacy benefit manager, such as Medco Health Solutions, since prices tend to be 10 percent lower than at retail. It's more convenient, too!

- **Kids mean more paperwork . . . am I keeping track of my receipts?** Household paperwork piles up even higher once kids enter the picture. Go through your medical receipts and make sure you've submitted all of your family's bills to your insurance company for reimbursement. This may sound pretty obvious, but any parent running a household knows that it's pretty easy to let things slip through the cracks. If dad takes a child to the pediatrician but doesn't normally handle the health insurance, he could easily stuff a bill in his work bag and never think about it again. (This has happened in my house!)

You should also go through all of your paperwork to make sure that you've been reimbursed to the full level you're entitled to. As we juggle jobs, kids and countless errands, billing errors are often overlooked and we just accept what an insurer tells us. But finding and fighting such an error can save you big bucks.

- **Kids change my family's needs . . . did I consider my options during open enrollment?** The plan that worked for you when you were single or even a couple isn't necessarily the right one for your growing family. Fifty-one percent of workers with health insurance have at least two health plans to choose from, according to the Kaiser Family Foundation. During open enrollment, make sure you consider your options.

  Also, if both spouses work, it may pay for each to go on his or her own employer's health insurance. Companies often penalize workers when they add a spouse to their health insurance. As a result, it's sometimes cheaper to have a spouse and the kids on one plan and the other spouse on his own employer's plan. Companies respect that you have kids; they just don't want to offer coverage to other adults, especially adults who work for someone else.

- **With my focus on my kids . . . am I still taking care of myself?** It's easy for parents to neglect their own health when taking care of small children. While it may be tough to find time to go to the gym, your employer may still try to make it worth your while. Companies are obsessed with lowering their costs, and they know that workers who are overweight or smoke can lead to larger medical bills. As a result, nearly 70 percent of companies are planning or already offer their workforce financial incentives for participating in wellness programs, according to benefits consulting firm Watson Wyatt Worldwide and the National Business Group on Health.

Call your human resources department to see if you're missing out on some of these discounts, ranging from a subsidized gym membership to lower insurance premiums.

USE YOUR PRETAX DOLLARS

If you have access to a flexible spending account through your employer or health savings account through a high-deductible health plan, you'd be smart to use it. As mentioned in Chapter 3, these accounts allow employees to set aside pretax dollars for out-of-pocket medical expenses ranging from co-payments to cough syrup. Most companies let their employees contribute up to $5,000 a year, allowing the average worker to save up to $2,000. Yet, as great as these accounts are, only about 20 percent of eligible folks take advantage of them, according to benefits administrator WageWorks.

Before you contribute the maximum allowed amount into an FSA, estimate how much your family will spend on health care over the next year. The one downside with these plans is that any money you put into an account that's not spent at the end of the year is gone forever.

An HSA, however, is a bit less risky, since unused contributions can roll over from one year to the next. With one of these accounts, families could consider contributing more than they need in a given year if they anticipate expenses that may exceed the allowed contribution, such as the birth of a child, in a future year.

THE WRITE-OFF

In a particularly bad year of high medical costs, add up your expenses to see if you can deduct them from your taxes. Be warned, this is no easy task. The IRS only allows you to deduct health care expenses that exceed 7.5 percent of your adjusted gross income.

One final thought about your health care: while getting everyone in your family to all of their regular checkups may feel expensive, it's a whole lot cheaper than waiting for an illness to strike and then needing more acute care. Your best bet is to get acquainted with your health plan and use it as effectively as possible.

CHAPTER 8

PAYING FOR HARVARD

Common Misconception:

I need to make saving for my children's college education my top financial priority.

The Reality:

Yes, it's important to start setting some money aside for college as early as you can. But it's even more important that you first save for your own retirement.

The Bottom Line:

Even if, after saving for retirement, you can only afford to set aside a little money each month into a college savings account, you'll still accumulate a nice sum that can be put toward school tuition.

If there's one thing parents think they should save for, it's their children's college education. In eighteen years, a degree from a public school will cost around $200,000 and a private university will run closer to $400,000, according to the College Board, which administers the SAT standardized college admissions test. For most of us, the only way to accumulate that kind of cash is to start setting money aside while our kids are still in diapers.

Todd Young, a father of two from Norwood, Massachusetts, says he started setting money aside for his first daughter when she was just eighteen months old. "Knowing where college costs are going, I don't think we'll be able to fully fund it," he says. "But at least we are giving her a head start." Sure, the Youngs could probably funnel a little more into their children's college savings account, but they are rightly focusing on funding their own retirement first.

That's because parents need to balance their desire to save for their children's college education with their other goals, particularly retirement. It's been said before, but it's worth repeating: your kids can take out loans for school, but you can't borrow for your golden years. So you need to first make sure that you're saving enough to live comfortably once you stop working. Then, you should look at your finances and figure out what you can afford to put toward a future tuition bill.

Don't get discouraged if you can't set aside as much as you had initially hoped. Even if you can save only $100 a month, it will make a difference and be worth the trouble. In eighteen years, that monthly contribution could be worth nearly $46,000 if you invest it in a tax-advantaged college savings account that makes at least 6 percent a year. Save $200 a month and the sum jumps to an impressive $91,000.

Remember: parents on any budget can come up with a college savings plan. It may not fully fund four years of tuition, especially if you have multiple children, but there are many financial solutions available for college.

THE STARTING LINE

Ask new parents what their biggest financial concern is and they're likely to say saving for college. The cost of tuition is daunting, to say the least. And if those same parents are motivated, they will start stashing away cash into a college savings account right away. A mistake many of these couples make is that they try to figure out how much they will need to save for tuition and make reaching that goal their first financial priority.

THREE STEPS TO SAVING FOR COLLEGE

Below I'll walk you through how to figure out how much to save for college, how to best stash away the money, and what to expect in terms of financial aid or loans if your education nest egg falls short.

Step 1: Set Realistic Goals

We all want to help our children get a college degree. But first you need to figure out how much you can realistically afford to save. (The good news is that even if you can't afford to stash away as much as you would like, if you save strategically, it will provide more than you realize.)

Step 2: Select a Savings Vehicle

Now it's time to figure out where to put the money you save. In this section, I'll walk you through the different savings options available to parents, including 529 plans, Coverdell education savings accounts and custodial accounts.

Step 3: Plan Now for Future Aid

The reality is that most families won't be able to cover all the expenses for college, especially if you have multiple children. Even though college is many years off, it's helpful to get a basic understanding now of how financial aid works and a handle on what steps you can take in the meantime to qualify for the most aid later on.

Then there are the parents who go to the other extreme. They feel college is so many years off that there's no reason to start planning for it now. Their first concern is funding nursery school, birthday parties and the occasional babysitter.

Both approaches are wrong, and could either derail your retirement plans or saddle both parents and kids with thousands of dollars in unnecessary loans. Instead, families need to

PRESCHOOL AND MORE

College isn't the only education expense you'll encounter as parents. The first big one is preschool. The average full-time nursery school costs between $3,400 and $10,800 a year, according to the National Association of Child Care Resource and Referral Agencies. But if you want to send your little Einstein to a highly competitive private program in a big city, you could end up spending upward of $30,000 a year. Fortunately, there are alternatives worth exploring that can save you money while still preparing your toddler for kindergarten.

Delay school. There's no reason your two-year-old needs a formal education. Instead, consider waiting until your daughter is three or even four and save a year or two of tuition.

Consider a co-op. Preschool cooperatives are often considerably cheaper than private preschools since they require parents to volunteer in the classroom.

Check out a parochial school. A preschool run by a church, synagogue or some other nonprofit organization is another cheaper alternative to a private school.

Research public programs. Money's often tight when families are just starting out. Don't be afraid to ask for financial assistance. Many preschools offer it. Also, according to the National Institute for Early Education Research, thirty-eight states offer public (read "free") preschool programs, although they may not be available in every school district. Twenty-seven of those states have income requirements for eligibility.

realize that saving for college is important but shouldn't be a family's number one priority, especially when there is financial aid available.

So how should parents approach their college savings? Start off by looking at your monthly budget. (If you don't already have one, the worksheet on page 186 can help you set one up.) After you've paid your mortgage and other living expenses, you'll likely have some money left over. Before earmarking it for college savings, you first need to direct funds to the following areas:

- **Retirement.** There are no loans for retirement. If you don't save for your own retirement, you'll have to keep working or lean on your children someday for support. That's why it's so important that you save for your golden years before you try to accomplish other financial goals. For most people that means contributing to an individual retirement account (either a Roth IRA or a traditional IRA) and maxing out your 401(k).

- **Insurance.** No one knows what the future will hold. That's why it's crucial you make sure your family is adequately insured with both life insurance and disability insurance. (I'll talk more about these two topics in Chapters 11 and 12.) Why? A death or loss of income can very quickly derail a family's ability to save for college. And without money coming in, cash you thought you would use for college may need to go toward your everyday expenses.

- **Eliminating high-interest-rate debt.** It's never a good idea to sit under a pile of high-interest-rate credit card debt. It's a better use of your money to pay off high-interest debt before you start saving for college. That's because your money over time may earn an average of only 7 percent to 10 percent (based on historical market returns) in a college savings account, while credit cards often carry interest rates of 15 percent or higher.

CHOOSING YOUR PIGGY BANK

There are better ways to save for college than hiding your money under a mattress. Here are some of the most common options.

529 Basic College Savings Plan

What it is. While there's no perfect savings vehicle, the 529 college savings plan is the best of the bunch. Named for the section of the Internal Revenue Code under which it was created, the 529 plan is a tax-advantaged savings account that allows you to invest money today and withdraw the funds free of federal income taxes, provided the money is used for qualified college expenses. Since there are no income limitations, anyone can open one.

How it works. A 529 plan looks and feels a bit like a 401(k). You contribute money into an account and have a basket of investment options to choose from. These accounts are operated by individual states and administered by fund companies such as TIAA-CREF and Fidelity. Parents can choose a plan from anywhere in the country, but some states offer additional tax advantages for residents, including income tax deductions, so it's a good idea to start out by considering your own state's offering. Since there are more than eighty plans out there, it's wise to research all of them before deciding which one is best for you, since fees and returns vary quite a bit. For help assessing different plans, check out SavingForCollege.com, an independent Web site that rates 529 plans.

Contribution limits. Limits vary by state with some allowing a total contribution of more than $300,000 per child. These figures, of course, are likely to increase as your children grow and the cost of college rises. On an annual basis, a parent is allowed to contribute $13,000 a year, or $26,000 for two parents. Or, if you happen to come into some extra cash, you can contribute $65,000 (or $130,000 for two parents) in a single year and then not make another contribution for five years.

The downside. If you overfund a 529 plan or your child doesn't go on to earn a bachelor's degree, you could be penalized.

Withdrawals not used for qualified college expenses are subject to taxes and a 10 percent penalty. If you got a state tax deduction, you'll have to report any money not used for college expenses as "recapture income" on your state tax return. The one saving grace is that if your kid chooses to become a rock star instead of going to college, you can always change the beneficiary to a younger sibling.

529 PREPAID TUITION PLAN

What it is. Your other 529 option is a prepaid tuition plan. It allows you to set aside money in an account that locks in today's tuition price for participating schools. These come in two flavors: state plans for state schools, and an independent 529 plan for private colleges.

State Plans

How state plans work. There are only a handful of states, including Florida, Virginia and Massachusetts, that offer prepaid programs. Generally, if you're fortunate enough to live in one of these states and think your child will go to school locally, they're worth considering. As the name implies, you are prepaying tuition at eligible schools in your state at today's prices. So whatever percentage of tuition you can cover today will apply to the future. (Rules vary greatly by state. Massachusetts' plan, for example, includes both state and some private schools and allows nonresidents to join.)

UPROMISE

Here's a freebie parents should consider taking advantage of: a no-charge service that helps you save for college with little effort. Members receive rewards—typically 1 percent to 3 percent—when they shop online, go out to eat, buy groceries or book travel with major merchants like Barnes and Noble, Target and Expedia. You can even get up to $3,000 if you buy or sell a home with certain real estate agents. The money you earn is collected into an account that you can link to a 529 plan. To sign up, log on to Upromise.com.

THE PUBLIC-VERSUS-PRIVATE DEBATE

Thinking about splurging and sending your children to a tony private elementary or high school? You're not alone. Eleven percent of children go to one, and interest in these programs is growing. Over the last decade, enrollment at independent elementary and high schools rose nearly 11 percent, according to the National Association of Independent Schools (NAIS). And it's safe to say that many more parents might want to opt out of the public school system if only there were more available private spots.

The decision of public versus private is a complicated and personal one for families. I'm not an educator, so I won't try to answer the question of what's best. I will, however, remind you to consider your finances before you write out that first tuition check.

Let's start by talking about the cost of a private education. The average tuition for the 2007–8 school year was $14,633 for elementary school and $18,287 for high school, according to NAIS. (And just like college costs, families should expect tuition to rise each year.) While financial aid is available, just 18 percent of private school students receive it, and the average grant totaled a little less than $11,000. Over twelve years, private school could cost you more than $200,000, without taking inflation into consideration.

Even if you can swing tuition, will spending all that money on private school put your college savings goals in jeopardy? If so, are you comfortable asking your child to take on more student loan debt than he may have been saddled with otherwise? Or will it force you to steer your son or daughter to a cheaper state school when it comes time to apply to college?

There are two potential solutions parents should think about. First, if you're absolutely set on giving your child a private school education, consider limiting it to just the high school years, when the intense college prep work really begins.

Or, if you simply don't have faith in your current school district, think about moving to a different area with a better school system. While the homes may cost more and you may need to downsize a bit, you'll actually be making an investment that could help pay for your retirement. Remember, real estate in good school systems tends to appreciate more than homes in poor school districts—that's an investment you can get back when you sell your house.

❧

Contribution limits. The same gift tax rules that apply to 529 plans apply to state prepaid plans. The lifetime limits are generally capped at four years of tuition.

The downside. If your child doesn't attend an eligible school, you can only get your money back with certain penalties. Again, rules vary greatly by state. In Florida, for example, the state will pay out the same amount of money it would apply to a public college if your child decides to go to a private Florida school or to school out of state. If you're in the Massachusetts plan and don't use the funds as planned, you'll get your money back plus the accrued interest at the rate of the consumer price index (CPI). The danger in this scenario is that the CPI tends to be lower than the rate of tuition inflation, so you might be left significantly short.

Independent 529

How the independent 529 plan works. The I529 is administered by the teachers' pension fund TIAA-CREF Intuition Financing and run by a consortium of the participating schools. Open an account and you can lock in current tuition prices at more than 270 private institutions, including highly competitive schools such as MIT and Princeton. As a bonus, you'll even get a slight discount off today's tuition, ranging between 0.5 percent and 4 percent. The one catch is that this program covers only tuition and some fees, so you'll have to save money in another account for room and board.

Contribution limits. Overall, you can contribute up to five years of tuition at today's prices. For the 2008–9 program year, that equals $183,000. On an annual basis, the same gifting rules apply to the I529 as the regular 529 college savings plan.

The downside. Your daughter could have her heart set on Yale or another great school not on the list. Or, there's also the chance that your son doesn't get into any of the participating schools he applies to. (Signing up for the program doesn't guarantee your child admission to any of the participating schools.) If that happens, you can get your principal back. But since this isn't an investment plan, you'll make a maximum of only 2 percent on your money, and that's far less than the historical stock market return. Another option: change the beneficiary to another child in the hopes that she chooses one of the member institutions. For more on this program, check out Independent529Plan.org.

Coverdell Education Savings Account

What it is. A Coverdell education savings account is a tax-advantaged plan that allows you to save for college as well as elementary and secondary school expenses. These accounts offer parents more investment options than 529 plans.

How they work. As with the 529 plan, your contributions grow tax free and withdrawals aren't taxed when used for qualified expenses. (Uncle Sam, however, does put some limitations on his generosity. If you're also claiming the Hope or Lifetime Learning credit in the same year, you may have to pay some tax on your Coverdell withdrawals.) There are also income limitations for opening an account. Contributions are phased out for parents who earn between $95,000 and $110,000 for single filers and $190,000 and $220,000 for joint filers.

Contribution limits. You can contribute up to $2,000 a year, but the annual limit is scheduled to drop to just $500 after 2010.

The downside. After 2010, these plans start to look less attractive. In addition to the contribution limits changing, parents will no longer be able to save for kindergarten through high school.

The UGMA and UTMA

What it is. Through the Uniform Gift to Minors Act (UGMA) and the Uniform Transfer to Minors Act (UTMA), a child can own securities and other investments in their own name as long as a parent or guardian acts as a custodian on the account until the child reaches the age of majority.

How they work. Parents can open an UGMA or UTMA custodial account at any financial institution. These accounts used to be very popular back when the earnings were taxed at the child's tax bracket. Parents were able to transfer stocks to their children and then pay only a very small amount of tax on the income that was generated. However, as we learned in Chapter 4, the so-called kiddie tax rules changed in 2008, and now a child's income above $1,900 is taxed at the parent's higher income bracket until age nineteen (or twenty-four if the child is a student).

Contribution limits. There are no lifetime limits on how much parents can contribute. If, however, you give your child more than the gift tax laws allow, $13,000 (per parent per year), the amount will go toward your $1 million lifetime allowance. Any amount over that is subject to taxes.

The downside. These accounts don't offer any of the tax advantages that you get with a 529 plan or a Coverdell education savings account. Parents also lose control over the money once their child reaches majority, which is twenty-one in most states. Finally, you can't transfer the assets to another beneficiary if your child decides not to go to college. (There are no penalties if the funds aren't used for college expenses.)

CRUMMEY TRUST

What it is. A Crummey trust is like an UGMA or UTMA custodial account, only it allows you to delay the age when your son or daughter inherits the money.

How it works. You typically need a lawyer to help you draft a Crummey trust. Every time you make a contribution, you need to notify your child and allow him or her to withdraw the money within a certain period of time, say, thirty days. If he or she doesn't drain the account, the control shifts back to the trustee until your son or daughter reaches the age you determine.

Contribution limits. The gift tax laws apply to Crummey trusts. There is no lifetime limit on contributions. Withdrawals can be spent on anything.

The downside. Your child could spend his college money on a Harley-Davidson and other toys long before he gets to campus. You also can't change the beneficiary of the account.

FINANCIAL AID 101

If you have small children, it's very difficult to know what your finances will look like in fifteen or eighteen years. But unless you're in a very high-paying job, chances are your family will need at least some financial assistance to help foot the tuition bill. According to the College Board, the good news is that the majority of families qualify for financial aid or subsidized loans.

And during the 2007–8 academic year, more than $143 billion in financial aid was given out to students, according to the College Board.

GRANTS

Pell grants. These are highly coveted government grants that don't need to be paid back. They are awarded to low-income students based on financial need. As generous as Pell grants are, however, they won't foot your child's entire tuition bill. (The maximum award for the 2009–10 award year was $5,350.) If you're particularly needy, your child may also qualify for Federal Supplemental Educational Opportunity Grants, which could add a few more thousand dollars in grant money to the total financial aid package.

State grants. If you attend a private or public school in your state, you may qualify for a need-based state grant. Some states even have reciprocal agreements with other states that let you take your aid with you.

WHO DOESN'T QUALIFY FOR FINANCIAL AID?

You have to be rather well off not to receive any financial aid. In today's dollars, the only families that wouldn't get any aid at a private university are those earning over $250,000 a year, says Reecy Aresty, a financial aid consultant and author of *How to Pay for College Without Going Broke*. Folks earning between $150,000 and $200,000 per year probably wouldn't receive any money from a public school, he says.

Families that don't qualify for financial aid can still take out federal loans to help pay for college. Students can also pursue merit-based scholarships or scholarships through a parent's employer or community organization.

Merit grants. Good students may also qualify for merit-based state grants, regardless of income.

For more on applying for grants, check out the government's Web site College.gov or FinAid.org.

FEDERAL WORK-STUDY

Many students will need to work their way through school. The federal work-study program provides part-time jobs to help those who need to earn money for books and other education expenses. The pay must match the federal minimum wage, but it could be higher. To learn more about work-study, check out the U.S. Department of Education's Web site at ed.gov.

SCHOLARSHIPS

School-based. Colleges give out more than one billion dollars each year to attract gifted athletes and exceptional students.

Private scholarships. Every year there are 2.9 million scholarships given out, worth a total of over $16 billion, according to lender Sallie Mae. Thanks to many Web-based search engines including those on SallieMae.com and FastWeb.com, it's easier than ever for students to find appropriate scholarships and apply. Common sources of scholarship money include a parent's employer, community organizations and corporations. Students as young as freshmen in high school can start applying for these rewards.

LOANS

Federal Perkins loans. These are low-interest-rate loans for low-income students. They come with no fees beyond the interest rate, and full-time students don't have to start repaying them until nine months after they graduate.

Stafford loans. There are two types of Stafford loans, subsidized and unsubsidized. If a student qualifies for a subsidized Stafford loan, the government pays the interest on the loan while he's in school. Students must pay all of the interest on an unsubsidized loan.

Plus loans. There's a government loan program for parents, too. The interest rate is typically higher than on Stafford loans but can usually help families fill in the gaps when Stafford loans aren't sufficient.

Private loans. Finally, there are loans available from private lenders that can help families fill in any remaining gaps in school expenses that weren't covered by grants and government loans. But the interest rates on these loans do tend to be higher.

For more on loans, check out the government's Web site for student aid at StudentAid.ed.gov. Lender Sallie Mae (SallieMae.com) and the College Board (CollegeBoard.com) are also useful resources.

GETTING THE MOST AID FOR YOUR INCOME

While you can't apply for financial aid now, you can do a few simple things to maximize the assistance your family receives later on. Financial aid is determined by a complex calculation of your assets, and there are certain types of accounts the federal government and schools don't consider when looking at the money you have available for tuition. Your goal is to stash away as much as you can in the most favorable way.

WHAT THE SCHOOLS WON'T TOUCH

Retirement accounts. Schools don't expect you to give up your nest egg for your child's education. But you can't just earmark any account as retirement; only a 401(k), IRA or some other qualified retirement account is exempt. In other words, your Charles Schwab day trading account doesn't count.

Your house. If your child attends a state school, your home equity is considered off-limits. If he goes to a private school, you may be expected to dip into some of your equity, although the amount varies by institution. If you're confident your kid is going to a state school, you could use your cash to pay off your mortgage.

INCREASE YOUR FINANCIAL AID

Think carefully when setting up a college savings account. Under the current federal financial aid rules—which could change—children are expected to contribute 20 percent of their assets toward tuition and fees (also known as the expected family contribution), while parents only have to fork over less than 6 percent before financial aid kicks in. To maximize how much money your family qualifies for, parents should save as much as they can in their own name, rather than their child's.

When you open a 529 college savings plan or a Coverdell education savings account, these accounts are viewed as parental assets and only 6 percent is expected to go toward school each year. Open an UGMA or UTMA account for your child and the accounts are considered the student's property; 20 percent of the assets are earmarked for tuition and fees. (Warning: if you try to protect funds in an UGMA or UTMA account by rolling them into a 529, the money is still considered your child's asset.)

———

Because the rules and programs surrounding college savings are constantly in flux, even after you set up your child's college savings plan, you must revisit it from time to time; there may be strategies you can implement or new products worth taking advantage of.

PART THREE

YOUR
CONTINGENCY
PLAN

CHAPTER 9

YES, YOU NEED A WILL

Common Misconception:

If your spouse dies, you'll be fine since you'll automatically inherit his or her assets.

The Reality:

You may need to ask your children for an allowance to help make ends meet. Without a will, most states divide the assets between the surviving spouse and the kids.

The Bottom Line:

Draft a will with your spouse before or soon after your first child is born. Specify how you want your assets distributed if one or both of you should pass away.

Want to be a good parent? Reading to your children every night and teaching them to eat their vegetables is a good start. But if you want to be a truly great mother or father, you'll also need to secure your family's future should anything happen to you or your partner. In this last section, I'll show you how to do just that by outlining the four tools every parent needs: a will, a trust, life insurance and disability insurance.

First, let's start with the will, which I consider the most important document in your arsenal. Here's a little-known fact:

Should your spouse die, you won't necessarily inherit all of his or her assets. Without a will, many states divide the assets between the surviving spouse and the children. The kids' portion is then administered by a court-appointed guardian under court supervision until the children reach age eighteen or twenty-one—it varies by state, warns Joanne Sternlieb, an estate-planning attorney based in New York City. You may then have to go through the hassle of requesting the money from the guardian to help pay for their living or school expenses. Either way, the harsh reality is that Mom or Dad may have to raise the brood on far less than anyone bargained for.

DYING WITHOUT A WILL

When you die without a will, your assets are distributed under state intestacy laws. To find out what would happen to your assets, contact an estate-planning attorney in your state. To get an unofficial opinion of how your assets would get split between your spouse and children, check out the Web site MyStateWill. com. It has an intestacy calculator that can be customized for every state.

As if that's not bad enough, without a will, a judge decides who gets custody of your children should something happen to both parents. While a judge may try to honor verbal agreements made between, say, a father and his sister, without written documentation it's awfully hard for your desired caregiver to prove what your wishes were. You should also expect family members to fight for custody. That means there's a chance your kids could end up with the last person you wanted to be their guardian.

The best time to set up a will is before you even give birth. But don't kick yourself if you haven't already drafted one. According to *Consumer Reports,* only 44 percent of adults have drafted a will (including a lot of parents with kids who are older than yours). The most important thing is to draft one as soon as possible and to update it every few years as you have more children and other changes occur in your family. While

PROTECTING A CHILD WITH SPECIAL NEEDS

According to the U.S. Census Bureau, approximately 4 percent of families are raising a child with a disability. If you're one of them, you'll need to take special care to provide for your son or daughter. In addition to drafting a will, you should also consider writing a letter of intent to help your child's guardian take better care of your little one's health and happiness.

In this letter, you'll want to address your child's unique medical history and include all of the contact information for his various doctors. You'll also want to write down details of his daily life; if your child has special routines he likes to follow or activities he enjoys, include them. Your goal is to pass along all the small details of your kid's life that he may not be able to express for himself.

You'll also want to discuss your child's financial situation. Many kids with special needs will never be able to earn a living as an adult and won't be able to pay for their own costly medical care. Fortunately, there are public benefits that can help, including Supplemental Security Income (SSI) and Medicaid. During your planning, you should speak with a lawyer to make sure you don't inadvertently make your child ineligible for those government programs. Bernard Krooks, an estate-planning attorney based in New York City, says that in some cases it's useful to set up a special-needs trust, which is designed to supplement but not replace any public benefits.

To find an estate-planning attorney who specializes in people with special needs, contact the Special Needs Alliance at 877-572-8472.

no one likes to face his or her mortality, you shouldn't let your own fears get in the way of protecting your family.

WHY PARENTS DON'T DRAFT WILLS

One of the most common reasons parents put off drafting a will is because it just seems too morbid and depressing.

STEPS FOR DRAFTING A WILL

1. Select a guardian and backup guardian for your children.

2. Choose an executor and backup executor for your will.

3. Ask guardians and executors if they are comfortable filling these roles.

4. Draft your will with the help of an estate-planning attorney or a software program such as Quicken WillMaker.

5. Write letters expressing your wishes to the guardians and executors.

6. Find two witnesses (some states may require more) to sign your will and make it legal.

7. Place your will in a safe place and tell your executor where to find it.

Reminder: you'll need to update your will every few years or when you have a major change in life, including the birth of another child or if you move to another state.

Perhaps if you don't think about dying, it won't happen, right? Fortunately, there's a very slim chance you'll even need a will while your children are young. But in the unfortunate event that something should happen to you, not having a will can only make things more tragic.

Not being able to decide whom to name guardian is another big reason parents avoid wills. The reality is that this is one of the harder decisions parents need to make. It can also be a very sensitive issue for couples to discuss, since it can bring up all sorts of feelings about each other's in-laws.

Fiona Schaeffer, a corporate attorney in New York City, and her partner have avoided drafting their will for this very reason. "If there's anyone who should know how important a will is, it's a lawyer like me," says Fiona. Rather than debate the merits of one relative over another, the couple has simply put off the task despite having a toddler and a second baby on the way.

While these conversations can feel like they're rocking a marriage during the already stressful time of adjusting to parenthood, you'll feel much better once you've named a guardian and have a will. Think of it this way: all those pre-natal tests were far from pleasant, but you went through with them for your child's well-being. Drafting a will is just as important.

THE NAME GAME

Todd Young, whom you met in Chapter 8, and his wife, Caryn, decided to draft their wills a few months after their first child was born. The Norwood, Massachusetts, couple wanted to make sure they had chosen a guardian to care for their children in case they couldn't—and they weren't willing to leave the decision to a judge.

After much thought, the Youngs decided to name Todd's older sister as guardian since she has two daughters and is raising them in the Jewish faith, which is very important to the couple. Knowing they have now settled the guardian issue gives the couple peace of mind.

Although it was easy for the Youngs to select a guardian, many couples, like Fiona and her partner, whom you met earlier in the chapter, struggle with this decision. If you're lucky, you'll have siblings and parents (and maybe even some friends) who will start campaigning for custody once they hear you're thinking of drafting your will.

The most important thing to remember is that this is your decision, and you're going to base it on what's best for your children. It would be a huge mistake to name a guardian simply because you're afraid of hurting someone's feelings. You may even come across the well-meaning relative who tries to bully you into naming her guardian. My best advice: smile and quickly change the subject. After all, who wouldn't prefer talking about reality TV rather than your demise?

What if that pushy relative persists? You have no choice but to have an honest conversation about your wishes. While the talk may be a bit uncomfortable, it's better to have some hurt feelings now than to have your loved ones argue about your intentions should you pass away. Also, point out that just because you aren't naming your family member as the guardian, it doesn't mean you don't want her to be a part of your children's lives. Create another role for that sibling or parent that makes her feel special. For example, if your sister likes to travel, ask her to take your kids on a special trip each year.

Here's how you should select a guardian and backup guardian. First off, you want to find someone who is responsible and shares your values. This will help ensure that your children are brought up in a fashion similar to how you would do it. For instance, if you want your daughters brought up with firm boundaries, you probably don't want to choose a relative who imposes few rules and believes a little chaos is a healthy part of childhood.

If you're lucky enough to have a few good options, consider these guidelines to help you narrow down your list. Many parents prefer guardians who have children of their own. The thinking here is that those other parents won't need to drastically change their lifestyle to accommodate more kids. A guardian without offspring of his own, on the other hand, may resent having to stay home on a Friday night.

When my husband and I decided to choose a guardian, it came down to my sister, Karen, and my husband's sister, Stefanie. We chose Karen because she has a son and Stefanie doesn't have any children; it just didn't seem fair to burden Stefanie with a lifestyle she hasn't yet chosen. In a few years when my sister's son goes off to college and my sister-in-law has a child, then we will likely change our wills.

Money is another important factor to consider. Can your chosen guardian afford to raise more children? Will he need to move to accommodate your kids? If so, are you willing to provide him with the money to do so? If at all possible, you don't want your little ones to be a financial burden causing stress in a new household. (I'll talk more about providing funds for a guardian in the next chapter, on trusts.)

Finally, it can be very stressful on children to move after losing their parents. Choosing a local guardian so the kids can stay in the same schools is an added plus. And your backup guardian is simply your second choice.

MULTIPLE GUARDIANS

There are times when parents may wish to name separate guardians for different children. This often happens in blended families with children from different marriages. Before you make any decisions, think carefully about how disruptive it will be for the children to not only lose their parents but also their siblings.

CHOOSING AN EXECUTOR

Now you need to choose your executor and a backup executor. The executor is the person who will pay all the debts and taxes and then redistribute your remaining property as dictated in the will. Since children under the age of eighteen typically can't own property on their own, the executor in many cases is also named the custodian or trustee (if you set up a trust) of the assets. This person should be trustworthy, good with money and willing to distribute the child's money the way you want. For example, if you want the bulk of the money to go toward your son's college education, the executor, if acting as the custodian for your son's assets under the Uniform Transfer to Minors Act, has to be able to say no to the guardian if he wants money to go on vacations.

Naming two different people as guardian and executor (if acting as custodian) is a good way to avoid any conflict of interests. It's also nice because the person best suited for carrying out the details of your will may not make a great guardian; your warm and fuzzy sister would do a much better job of raising the kids, while your meticulous brother is your best choice for making sure your affairs are in order. And while you may not feel comfortable choosing someone outside the family to act as guardian, it's an option worth considering when naming an executor. We chose my husband's oldest and most trusted friend.

ASKING PERMISSION

YOUR FINANCIAL PLAN

It's important to plan for your children's financial future in the event that you and your spouse are not around to support them. Any assets you have now, including a home or a retirement account, can go toward helping a guardian raise them. Most parents, however, will also need to purchase life insurance, especially if they want to provide their kids with a college education. I'll discuss buying life insurance in Chapter 11.

You should always make sure that whomever you've chosen to act as guardian (and backup guardian) and executor (and backup executor) are on board with your plan. You're likely to find that most people are flattered that you've chosen them. But some others, especially potential guardians, may be concerned about having enough money to raise a couple of extra kids. Now is the time to discuss your financial plan with your chosen guardian and how much money you expect to provide for them to raise your children. In the best-case scenario, you'll have enough life insurance that your children won't be an added financial burden for anyone.

You'll also want to inform your backups that they're named in your will. This could get a little touchy, of course, since you're basically telling them that they're your second choice. Try to explain your decision as logically as possible. I explained to my sister-in-law that I didn't want to burden her young marriage with children before she was ready. As for the remaining relatives you didn't choose, there's really no reason to explain anything to them. Most likely your wishes will never be read while your children are young and your mother will never need to know that you rejected her.

DRAFTING YOUR WILL

Now it's time to make it legal. If you have a relatively simple estate, you can probably draft your own will with the help of a software program like Quicken WillMaker. Then, you just need to find two witnesses to sign the document and you're done. (Since laws vary, check with your state for its requirement.)

If you think your estate is a bit on the more complicated side (maybe you anticipate having to pay estate taxes), you'll want to get a lawyer involved. The good news here is that a lawyer can also help you create all sorts of useful documents, including a trust, living will, medical directive and power of attorney. A lawyer's time doesn't have to be expensive. The tab could easily be kept under $1,000 if all you're doing is setting up a will. Expect to spend a few thousand if you want a complete estate plan.

> **WHEN TO CALL AN ATTORNEY**
>
> 1. Your estate (including life insurance) could get hit with estate taxes.
> 2. You have a special-needs child.
> 3. You desire complex estate-planning advice.
> 4. You want to make sure you don't make any mistakes that could make your will invalid.

Now for the logistics. Just because you and a partner have a child together doesn't mean that you'll want to write a joint will. In most cases each parent will want to draft his and her own documents. The danger with writing up a joint will is that the decisions the two of you make will stand as long as either of you are alive. So should one of you pass on at an earlier age, the other one won't be able to make any changes to the will, even if life circumstances for the survivor change.

You want to keep your will as simple and straightforward as possible. The first thing it should address is whom you want

WILL YOU GET HIT WITH ESTATE TAXES?

Worried your estate might trigger the dreaded estate tax? The trouble is that no one knows what the estate tax rules will look like in a few years. Here are the current federal exemption levels, which are subject to change at any time. (Many states also impose an estate tax.)

2009: If your estate is larger than $3.5 million, it will trigger the estate tax.

2010: There are no estate taxes for this year.

2011: The estate tax is reinstated for all estates over $1 million.

Don't confuse drafting a will with planning your estate. While a will is a necessary component of estate planning, it won't keep you from paying needless estate taxes. An estate-planning attorney can walk you through all of the necessary documents you'll want to consider, including a trust, living will, medical directive and power of attorney.

to leave your property to. Many married couples leave everything to each other should just one person pass away, and then everything to their children should both parents die at the same time. You should name who gets what if there are special heirlooms that you want to distribute.

Finally, you will have to decide what happens to your assets should you and your spouse and children all pass away. My husband and I decided that we would each get half of the total assets to distribute how we liked. We each chose family members based on need and then each allocated large chunks of money to our favorite charities.

Although you've already asked your guardian and executor to act on your behalf, it's essential to name them in your will so there's no question as to whom you want in those roles.

MARRIED WITH ASSETS

As if estate planning wasn't complicated enough, it turns out that some of your assets pass outside of your will. That means that whomever you name as your designated beneficiary on your retirement plan, life insurance or brokerage accounts will inherit your money no matter what your will says. (Joint assets, including joint bank accounts with a pay-on-death provision, also pass outside of a will.) People often name parents and siblings as beneficiaries on retirement accounts when they start jobs, if they aren't yet married, and they often forget to change them. The other common error is not taking a former spouse off an account after a divorce. What are the chances that your ex will do the right thing and hand over your life insurance money to the new Mrs.? The bottom line: your will doesn't override beneficiary designations on all accounts, so make sure all your paperwork is up to date.

If you choose not to create a trust for your children, you also need to name a custodian, who will then manage your children's property. And as I mentioned earlier, most states require two witnesses who aren't named in the document to sign your will whether you use a lawyer or not. Some states also require a self-proving affidavit, which is usually signed in front of a notary public.

Once the will itself is finished, you'll want to write letters to the guardians, executors and custodians so that they know your wishes in detail and can care and provide for your children in the way you would like. (You can find a sample letter on page 136.) Then put those letters and your will in a secure place in your home, such as a fireproof and waterproof safe. Your attorney should also keep a signed copy of the document.

SAMPLE LETTER TO GUARDIAN

Dear Denise,

Thank you for taking on the responsibility of caring for our daughter. As you know, she means more to us than anything in the world. While we hoped this day would never come, it gives us comfort to know that Abigail is with you.

When we chose you as guardian, we felt comfortable knowing that you share many of the same values that we do and will make choices for Abigail similar to those we would have made. Having said that, we'd like to offer some thoughts on how we would like her raised.

As you know, family is very important to us. We hope that you will encourage Abigail to embrace the love of family. In addition to your side of the family, we hope that you will help Abigail maintain a close relationship with the other side as well. We want her to have a close relationship with all of her aunts, uncles and grandparents. We hope that she will spend holidays and visit regularly with them.

Education is also very important to us. We hope Abigail will apply herself in school and go on to a high-quality university and perhaps even graduate school. Please keep on top of her grades and help her understand why a solid education is an important foundation for her future.

Since we both had varied interests while we were young, we would also love you to help Abigail find her interests. Please encourage her to learn an instrument, take dance lessons or pursue whatever hobby she enjoys. We want her life to have as much richness as possible.

We also think it could be good for you to encourage Abigail to go to sleep-away summer camp and travel with other family members. For you, we hope this will provide a much-needed break from child care. And for her, we think it will help her learn to be independent and expand her perspective.

Finally, we tried to prepare financially as much as possible for this day. If we did our math right, Abigail should be no financial strain for you. We named Alan Smith as the trustee for Abigail's trust and hope that the two of you can work together to support her. We gave Alan quite a bit of leeway to give you the money you need. But we also want to make sure that cash isn't spent on non-necessities if it would put her college fund in jeopardy. Since we can't be here to help Abigail with her school expenses, we want to know that her tuition is taken care of and that she should be able to graduate debt-free. We'd also like to hope that there's a little something left over, so she has a security cushion when she does graduate, since we won't be able to give her the financial help that so many parents give young graduates.

Thank you for taking care of our baby as you would your own.

Love,
Lynn and Harris

A bank safe deposit box can be a bad place to keep a will. Some states require family members to get a court order to open the box if you pass away.

Now you can take a deep breath because you've just completed the most important part of your contingency plan. In the next chapter, we'll go over when drafting a trust makes sense.

CHAPTER 10

TRUSTS:
THEY AREN'T
JUST FOR THE
WEALTHY

Common Misconception:

Trusts are only for rich people.

The Reality:

Without a trust, your brother could spend all of your hard-earned money on a new boat rather than shoes for the kids.

The Bottom Line:

Don't procrastinate. Set up a trust before or soon after your baby is born. This way you'll be able to control how your assets are spent and at what age your children will inherit your money.

You don't need to be Bill Gates to consider setting up a trust for the kids; even middle-class folks benefit from trusts when it comes to estate planning. That's because children under the age of eighteen can't directly inherit more than a small amount of money. So if you have more than that to leave to your minor child and make no provisions in your will, a court will appoint a property guardian to manage your child's assets until he reaches eighteen or twenty-one (depending on the state).

Here's the rub with that scenario: the property guardian may be a complete stranger; he won't understand your values. Perhaps more importantly, he could add one more layer of bureaucracy to an already complicated situation. When your child needs money, the guardian may have to make a formal request that then goes through the court system. It can be a real headache for your kids to get funds when they need it, and it's not an arrangement that's always in their best interests.

One way around the court system is to set up a custodial account for your kids through your will. In that case, you get to name the custodian, and she decides how the money is spent. Once your son or daughter is considered legally an adult (either eighteen or twenty-one, depending on state law, under the Uniform Transfers to Minors Act), he or she inherits the money outright. The problem with this setup is that Junior might blow through the money and have nothing left over for college.

For many parents, setting up a trust is a better alternative that allows them more control over how their money is spent once they're gone. If you have the means and want your child to go to private school, for example, include that in the trust document. A trust can also delay the age at which your kids get their hands on the money. This is often the biggest selling point for parents. Most people, looking back, would probably agree that they didn't necessarily make the most responsible decisions about money when they were eighteen or twenty-one, a time of life when it may have seemed perfectly reasonable to rack up credit card debt on pizza and beer. Even delaying a few more years—until, say, twenty-five, which is a common age for outright inheritance of a trust—makes the money more likely to be put toward, for example, graduate school or a down payment on a house.

While setting up a trust is a bit more complicated than a custodial account—a trust does require a lawyer's assistance—

it also provides more financial security for your children and is therefore worth considering. Ideally, you should set up a trust when you draft your will. But you can always add a trust later as your estate gets more complicated or your assets increase.

IS A TRUST RIGHT FOR ME?

Like many people, before I had a child, I thought trusts were only for the wealthy. I'm not wealthy, so I figured I would never need one. But then I had my daughter and we purchased enough life insurance to cover her basic living expenses and future college tuition. It suddenly hit me that while I may not feel like a Rockefeller now, my child stands to inherit a fairly large chunk of change if my husband and I both pass away. Chances are your children could inherit a fair bit of money, too, even if you aren't an investment banker.

While drafting a trust may initially feel like just one more thing that you don't have time for, you should think of it as another piece of your estate plan. If you're using a lawyer, it will simply feel like you're drafting a longer will. The following pages will help walk you through the process—it's not nearly as overwhelming as it may seem at first, and it can be a crucial tool for your children's financial protection.

KNOWING IF A TRUST IS RIGHT FOR YOU

As I said earlier, you don't need to be rich for your children to benefit from a trust. Here are a few questions to ask yourself that may help you figure out if a trust is right for your family.

1. Do you anticipate leaving your children more than a modest sum of money? (Are you leaving a life insurance policy for them?)

2. Do you want to have some say in how your children's money is spent?

3. Would you prefer that your children inherit the money after age eighteen or twenty-one?

4. Do you want the money to be used for a college education?

5. Would you like your children to have some kind of recourse if their money is mismanaged?

Let's start with the first question. A trust may not be worth the effort if you think you'll only be leaving a child (or children) $100,000 or less. Frankly, by the time a baby gets to college that hundred grand may cover only one year of expenses at a private university. On the other hand, if you're leaving life insurance money to cover four years of school and you own a home, there's a good chance a trust would make sense for you.

If you answered yes to question 2, a trust allows you to restrict spending to basic support, including food, clothing, education and health care. This is something that can't be done with a custodial account. If the custodian is a softie, he could end up lavishing your child with designer jeans and a fancy car, leaving very little left for her college years. Even worse, if the custodian is also the guardian, she could start writing herself large "support" checks to help cover her other expenses.

Regarding question 3, if you think giving a high school senior a large sum of cash is a recipe for disaster, then you should consider a trust. The ability to delay inheritance was the main draw for drafting a trust for Laurie and Greg Wetzel, a New York City–based couple in their mid-thirties with three small children. Should something happen to both of them, they decided that their kids will each inherit half of their inheritance at age thirty, and the remaining amount when they reach thirty-five. "Your twenties are such a transitional time that we don't want our children to have significant financial decisions to make," says Laurie Wetzel.

Greg was also concerned about their kids' maturity before reaching thirty. "I know personally that there are a lot of things

STEPS FOR DRAFTING A TRUST

1. Select a trustee and an alternate trustee.

2. Ask trustees if they are willing to act on your behalf and if they feel confident fulfilling the job's duties.

3. Decide at what age you want your children to directly inherit the money.

4. Draft the trust with the help of an estate-planning attorney.

5. Write letters expressing your wishes to your trustees.

6. Place your trust in a safe place with your will and tell the trustees where to find it.

7. Review your trust every few years to make sure it still matches your needs.

I appreciate in my thirties that I couldn't adequately appreciate about money in my twenties."

On the education front, if you specifically bought life insurance so that there would be enough money to help fund college in the event of your death, then you'll definitely want to delay the age at which your kids inherit your money. Otherwise, the risk is that your child could think a red Ferrari is a better investment than a crimson Harvard diploma.

Finally, one more benefit of a trust that you don't get with a custodial account is that a trust is a legal contract; the trustee has an obligation to follow your directions and act in a reasonable and prudent manner. If the beneficiary feels the trustee spent the money frivolously, he can demand what's called an accounting and sue for reimbursement if the trustee acted improperly with the funds. It may be pretty tough to prove illegal or improper actions with a trust, but sometimes just the threat of a possible lawsuit can keep someone in line.

CHOOSING A TRUSTEE

The trustee holds the purse strings, so don't delegate this job lightly. You need someone who is trustworthy, is good with money and has great attention to detail. In other words, don't choose your brother who has trouble remembering to pay his own bills on time or who starts breaking out in hives just thinking about April 15.

It's also important to remember that your trustee is going to be working with your guardian, so they had better get along. While they don't need to be best friends—in fact, it's probably better if they aren't—they also can't be archenemies. You want your trustee to be able to tell your guardian she can't use the money to buy your son a new sports car, but you also want your trustee to take your guardian's phone calls when she needs more money to pay for your son's braces.

Then there's the issue of naming a family member as your trustee. There's no general rule here, and many people—including the Wetzels—prefer to name a sibling since there's no one in the world they trust more. Siblings also typically don't charge to perform the service. On the other hand, my husband and I chose a close family friend. In our case, we felt he would be less biased and was more likely to follow through with our wishes without passing judgment on how we want our child's money spent. If you have significant assets, you could also hire a third party, such as a bank, to act as a trustee.

You'll also face the debate over naming your children's guardian as the trustee. On one hand, it's rather convenient. The person raising your kids won't have to ask anyone for permission about how the money will be spent. But on the other hand, a division of power can be a safer route. Some estate-planning attorneys worry that having one person fill the dual role leads to a conflict of interest and the risk that the guardian could take money for herself. Therefore, many lawyers recommend separating the two jobs. If nothing else, it also allows a second person to make sure that your wishes are carried out properly.

If you have a lot of money—more than a million dollars—you may want to name a bank or lawyer to act as trustee. An institution has a lot of experience handling accounts and taking care of all the investments and necessary tax paperwork. You could also offer your trustee the option to hire a bank and act as cotrustee or as an agent so that he or she still has ultimate control. This would lessen the burden for your named trustee but also allow him or her to sit in on meetings and help make decisions. He or she would basically keep an eye on the bank. Just be aware that a bank's services aren't free. They typically charge an annual fee of 1 percent to 2 percent of the principal.

TRUSTEE JOB DESCRIPTION

Naming someone a trustee is an honor, but it's also a lot of work. Most importantly, a trustee must follow your wishes as they're outlined in the trust document and abide by your state's laws. On an everyday basis, the trustee will need to work with your child's guardian to meet the beneficiary's financial needs. He will supervise the investment of the assets and make the distributions. The trustee will also need to file annual income tax returns. And finally, once the beneficiary reaches the age when she can inherit the money, the trustee will need to give her a full accounting of how the money was spent. Clearly, this isn't a task for someone who isn't organized and detail-oriented.

FULL DISCLOSURE

Most people have a pretty good idea of what it means to be a child's guardian, but that's not always the case with being a trustee. This job entails everything from investing money to filing tax returns—in other words, it's not much fun. If the trust isn't large enough to merit management by a bank, you can make this job a little less tedious for your chosen trustee by allowing him or her to hire a financial advisor or accountant to help out with the details.

SHOULD EACH CHILD HAVE A SEPARATE TRUST?

If you have a few small kids, your best bet is to create one family trust. First, it's easier for the trustee to manage. Also, if you start dividing up the money now, there could be a problem later on if one child develops special needs and requires more money than the others. Once the youngest child reaches age twenty-one, you can divide the money into separate trusts, says estate-planning attorney Joanne Sternlieb.

Individual trusts can make sense if there's a significant age difference between your children and you don't want the older one to have to wait to inherit his or her share until the younger one reaches maturity. Some families also choose separate trusts when there are children from different marriages involved.

❧

DRAFTING THE TRUST

Now that you've gotten this far, it's time to hire a lawyer or use the same one who drafted your will. An attorney may ask you to sign standard forms with boilerplate language, but don't feel locked in; you can personalize the trust to better meet your family's needs. For example, we decided to make some changes to New York's standard trust, which would have made our daughter's future spouse a cotrustee. Maybe it was my pregnancy hormones talking, but I got it in my head that I didn't want some unknown philandering husband to have any connection to this money. Divorce is too common. Why would we want to put our daughter's money in any kind of jeopardy?

As much as trusts are about maintaining some say in how your money is spent, you also need to provide vague enough language in the document to allow your trustee some leeway should your child's needs change or should something come up that you couldn't have anticipated. Tie the trustee's hands too tightly and the money could sit in a brokerage account

SAMPLE LETTER TO TRUSTEE

Dear Alan,

Thank you for taking on this responsibility and managing Abigail's assets until she's old enough to do so on her own. While we wish this day had never come to pass, we can take some comfort knowing that her finances and her future financial security will be well looked after by you.

Since acting as trustee is quite a time-consuming task, please feel free to hire a corporate trustee to act as cotrustee. We only ask that you remain involved to ensure that the assets are well managed and that Abigail's needs are met. The last thing we want is for a bank to act as a stumbling block for Abigail, denying her access to money that she needs or wants for reasonable requests, including piano lessons and school trips.

We chose Denise, my sister, to act as guardian. We have no doubt that Denise will welcome Abigail with an open heart into her home. But since adding an extra person to any family can be stressful, we want to smooth out any possible issues by making sure Abigail isn't a financial burden on Denise's household. Therefore, we would like the trust to pay out money each month for Abigail's basic care, medical needs and living expenses.

It's also important to us that Abigail enjoys life and gets to pursue after-school activities and hobbies. Provided there's enough money to go around after taking into consideration the future cost of college, we'd also love her to go to sleep-away camp. Some of Lynn's fondest memories come from her summer experiences away from home, and we also think it will provide Denise with some alone time with the rest of her family.

After Abigail's basic expenses, our main priority is for this money to go toward her college education (and living expenses while in school) and any graduate work she wishes to complete. Again, if money is available, we would also like to encourage her to travel during school and after she graduates, since we believe one can't learn everything one needs in life in the classroom.

We decided to delay the age Abigail will directly inherit these assets. Managing money is no small task, and we want to make sure she is mature enough to handle it. We also want to encourage her to pursue a career and learn to live independently. She will directly inherit half of the money at age twenty-five and the other half at age thirty-five. When she does eventually inherit the money, please try to guide her and set her off on a conservative fiscal path.

Finally, while it may seem a little silly now, we want to make sure that Abigail's money is shielded from her future spouse. While we would like to hope that she finds true love, we would hate for her to lose the one security blanket she has on the off chance that her marriage doesn't work out. Please explain to Abigail that she should always keep this money separate and never commingle it with her spouse's assets, since it could then be considered marital assets. (If the laws should change, please advise her appropriately.) Since we won't be around to help her out when things get difficult in life, we want to make sure she at least has her inheritance to fall back on.

One last thing: it's okay to be a bit generous with Abigail; we know we would have been. Just please make sure she retains a strong sense of the value of money and that there's plenty of it for her education, since it's the one thing in life she'll always be able to build upon.

Thank you again for taking care of our most precious daughter.

Sincerely,

Lynn and Harris

rather than paying for pricey cello lessons for a budding musical genius.

Finally, like you did for your guardian, you'll want to write your trustee a letter expressing your wishes for how you want the money spent on your children. Here you can provide some additional guidance. Some parents go so far as to say that some of the money can be used to help raise the living standard of the other kids in the house, so everyone feels equal. For example, if you want your son to go to sleep-away camp, but your sister can't afford to send her daughter, you could pay for her, too, so everyone gets along in the house. Of course, it's up to the trustee to then crunch the numbers and make sure there is still money left over for college, if that's your main goal.

CHAPTER 11

LIFE INSURANCE: BETTER SAFE THAN SORRY

Common Misconception:

Additional life insurance is too expensive. I'll be fine if I stick with the basic policy I have through my employer.

The Reality:

Your employer's plan isn't nearly enough. Plus, leave your job and you've just lost your life insurance, too.

The Bottom Line:

Fortunately, it's never been cheaper to buy life insurance on the open market. So buy as much term life insurance as you can afford. A thirty-five-year-old man can purchase a $500,000 policy for just $500 a year.

No one likes to think about life insurance, because it makes them think about their own demise. But unless you have enough money set aside *today* to comfortably support your family (and possibly pay for college), you had better seriously consider buying a policy. The good news is that you can purchase a lot of coverage for a relatively small sum. And

PREGNANCY AND LIFE INSURANCE

Despite the medical advances in childbirth, life insurance companies still consider it a risk to insure pregnant women. So if you're considering a second or third child and want to increase your coverage, make sure to do it before you conceive. If you're already pregnant, you may have to wait until after the baby is born to change your policy.

As for the fathers, there's no better time to buy a policy than before your partner gives birth. Sure, it would be easier just to buy two policies at once, but in this situation, a little extra hassle is worth the peace of mind—you can have your policy in place and your family protected as soon as possible. Besides, if you wait until after the baby is born, there's a good chance you'll put it off for months or even years as you get caught up in changing diapers and trying to manage erratic sleep schedules—both the baby's and yours.

agents are so hungry for your business that they actually go out of their way to make the process as painless as possible.

Long before my husband and I had a child, we bought our first life insurance policies. Once I became pregnant, increasing our coverage was easy. That's because we had already gotten over the fear of discussing the "what if I die" issue, and we knew exactly what type of life insurance we wanted: term life.

PREPARING FOR
THE UNTHINKABLE

The typical person buying life insurance is a forty-year-old man with a ten-year-old child, according to Byron Udell, the founder and chief executive officer of online insurance provider Accu-Quote. Why do parents wait so long to take care of something so important? "They don't want to deal with their own mortality issues," says Udell. "It isn't until they know someone who had breast cancer or a heart attack that it hits them that they need life insurance."

When Mona and Michael Berman, whom you met in Chapter 5, decided they wanted to start a family, they bought life insurance before Mona even got pregnant. That's because a very close friend had passed away suddenly—before he had a chance to finish filling out his life insurance paperwork. The friend's wife was five months pregnant and then faced the prospect of raising a child without her husband's income or insurance proceeds. Having witnessed this, Michael knew he didn't want to take any chances, and the Bermans sleep easier now knowing their child would be provided for.

The other reason people put off buying some coverage is because the process can seem so mind-numbing and confusing. According to the insurance trade group LIMRA, half of parents say they don't know how much life insurance to buy, and 39 percent worry about making the wrong decision when they do get around to purchasing a policy.

Not to worry—after reading this chapter you'll feel empowered and able to confidently buy your own life insurance.

DO I REALLY NEED LIFE INSURANCE BEYOND MY EMPLOYER'S PLAN?

Unless you're a successful hedge fund manager, chances are you need to buy life insurance. The reality is that a family's expenses only increase once children enter the picture, and in addition to the devastating emotional loss, most young families would feel a shattering financial blow if the main breadwinner was no longer contributing to the household. Twenty-two percent of families with dependent children admit they would have immediate trouble meeting everyday living expenses if the primary wage earner passed away, according to LIMRA. And 26 percent say they will be able to cover expenses for only a few months.

THREE STEPS FOR NAVIGATING LIFE INSURANCE

If the only thing standing in your way when it comes to your family's future is an insurance agent, these three steps will show you how to buy a highly rated policy online.

Step 1:
Evaluate Your Situation

There's always the possibility your family doesn't need life insurance, but unless you're fairly confident your assets can support your spouse and kids for the next 20 or so years, you'll probably want to consider purchasing a policy.

Step 2:
Select the Right Policy

Most young families are best off buying term life insurance, which provides coverage for a set number of years, since it offers the most coverage for the lowest price. But there are times when other products, including a whole life policy (which includes an investment component) or a return-of-premium policy, make sense. I'll define these types of products a little later and help you choose which one makes the most sense for your family.

Step 3:
Buy the Policy and Consider a Life Insurance Trust

Buying a policy is easy. You can call a local agent or start the process online. The important thing to remember is that life insurance is a bit of a commodity, so as long as a company is highly rated, it doesn't really matter which insurer you go with.

If you're buying a policy that could push the value of your estate to levels that trigger the estate tax, you'll want to consider a life insurance trust. Do this when you buy the policy, and the trust goes into effect immediately. Otherwise, you'll have a three-year waiting period before it goes into effect.

You may think that you already have some coverage through work, but I'm going to tell you now to imagine it doesn't exist. Here's why: the free life insurance your employer gives you vanishes the day you leave your job. (You may be able to convert it and bring it with you, but it's probably not worth the effort.) And since you never know when you could get laid off or need to leave voluntarily, you just shouldn't count on it. Most companies also don't provide you with much coverage. According to MetLife, the average company provides its employees with one to two times your salary, with a cap up to $50,000. That's not nearly enough money for a typical family's needs should it lose its primary breadwinner.

And even if you've already bought some life insurance in the past, you may need to increase it. Many couples purchase a policy when they buy a home or have their first child and don't think about their policies again. By the time the second or third baby arrives, they find they are significantly underinsured. That helps explain why 56 percent of married couples with children under eighteen believe they need additional life insurance, according to LIMRA.

To determine if you need to go out and purchase individual life insurance or increase your current coverage, you'll want to take a look at your family's balance sheet. Focus on your liquid assets, including your cash and investments. (You don't want to include your home unless you and your partner are comfortable selling it should anything happen to one of you.) Ask yourself if you have enough money for your partner and kids to live on for, say, the next twenty years.

The good news is that you don't need all of the money right now in liquid assets. But you do need to have enough to be able to live off of the income. So if you have $500,000, your family can conservatively count on investing it to generate about $25,000 annually. (This is based on a 5 percent return.) Is that enough for your family? If not, then you probably need life insurance.

DO ALL PARENTS NEED INSURANCE?

No. Life insurance is meant to replace income, so you usually only need to insure the breadwinners. If you're a two-income household and need both incomes to pay your bills, then both partners will need some coverage. If one parent works part-time and the income won't be missed, it may not be as necessary to buy that spouse a policy when you could put that premium toward other family savings goals.

However, there is one exception when you should insure a stay-at-home parent: when the working spouse's salary isn't enough to cover living expenses *and* child care. If that's the case, then the stay-at-home spouse may want to purchase a modest policy to help cover potential caregiver costs.

THE MAGIC NUMBER

Once you decide you need life insurance, you then have to figure out how much will adequately support your family. As a rule of thumb, you need eight to ten times your current annual salary, says Scott Simmonds, an independent insurance consultant based in Saco, Maine. So if you make $100,000, you should consider a $1 million policy.

While a $1 million policy may feel like a vast sum of money, it may not stretch as far as you imagine, especially if you're buying life insurance to help fund a college education. In eighteen years, a degree from a private university could cost upward of $400,000.

Young parents in their twenties and thirties who wish to maintain their current lifestyle without a stay-at-home mother or father returning to work may want to consider buying a policy worth twenty times their income, says AccuQuote's Byron Udell. He argues that buying so much coverage is the only way a family could replace that parent's entire paycheck for the next thirty years, assuming they live off the investment income from an insurance payout and it earns a 5 percent to 6 percent return.

CHOOSING THE RIGHT PRODUCT

The main debate when it comes to choosing life insurance is term life or whole life. But once you really start to study all of your options, you'll see that there are also variable life, universal life and return of premium.

Realistically, young families don't have the time or the patience to adequately research and weigh all of their choices. So let's keep this simple: if you're looking for the most coverage for the least amount of money, buy a term life insurance policy. Your goal is to replace any lost income your family may suffer should you pass away, so you want to buy a policy for a length of time that spans your working years. If you're in your mid-twenties, you may need to buy an additional policy about ten years down the road, since the longest policies you'll find last thirty years and won't get you to retirement.

Why is this a better choice than whole life insurance for most young families? Whole life combines basic life insurance coverage with a savings component, so in addition to providing your heirs with insurance coverage, the insurance company is also investing money on your behalf. While this can sound pretty appealing when a sales agent describes it to you, it's far too expensive for parents who are already having trouble making ends meet.

Consider: a thirty-five-year-old man (nonsmoker) could buy a thirty-year, $500,000 term life policy for just $440 a year, according to AccuQuote. But it would cost him $4,500 a year for that same amount of coverage on a whole life policy. What often ends up happening is that the family with whole life buys less coverage than it needs, because the premiums are so high, or the family starts paying those high premiums only to find they can't afford them and they cancel the plan.

The other problem with whole life is that these policies are weighed down with investment fees that make them a far more expensive way to invest your money versus a no-fee mutual fund. Most experts agree that if you're looking to set aside money for retirement, you're better off taking the difference between a term life policy and a whole life policy and investing the money on your own.

The only time it may make sense to buy a whole life plan is if you're wealthy and you're looking for ways to pay your estate taxes. Your financial planner or estate-planning attorney can tell you if this makes sense for your family.

Finally, there's a third option for some people who can't live with the feeling that they aren't getting anything in return for buying term life insurance (unless, of course, they pass away). If having the insurance when you need it isn't enough for you, you could consider what's called a return-of-premium policy.

Think of return-of-premium policies as a compromise between term life and whole life. You buy a policy for a set amount of time, and in the event that you pass away, your heirs are paid the face value of your death benefit. But should you outlive your policy, the insurer sends you a tax-free check for the full amount that you've spent on premiums. The downside? Price. It costs 50 percent more than a standard term policy.

MAKING THE PURCHASE

Now it's time to buy that policy. If you're the type of person who likes to have his hand held, you can call an insurance agent directly. Perhaps you have a friend who can make a recommendation. The large life insurance companies are also happy to refer you to a local agent in your area.

If you're a bit more independent, you can start the process online yourself with a Web site such as AccuQuote.com, InsWeb.com or TermAssist.com. You plug in some simple information, including your age and sex, and the software spits

HOW RISKY ARE YOU?

How much will life insurance cost your family? The good news is that term life policies are considered relatively inexpensive, although the actual price will vary depending on a number of factors.

First there is age. As you might expect, the younger you are, the less you'll pay for a policy. In 2008, a twenty-eight-year-old man in good health would pay $870 a year for a $1 million preferred thirty-year term life policy, according to AccuQuote. A thirty-eight-year-old man would pay $1,165 a year for the same policy.

Then there is whether or not you're a smoker. Smokers will pay a lot more. Let's go back to the twenty-eight-year-old buying a thirty-year, $1 million term life policy. A smoker will pay $2,335, or more than two and a half times as much as the nonsmoker.

That brings us to your risk class: preferred plus, preferred and standard. (Some insurance companies will have lower ratings, including substandard.) People ranked preferred plus will pay the least, while those who are considered standard will pay the most. The same twenty-eight-year-old nonsmoker would save $210 on his annual premium if he scored a preferred plus premium; he'd also pay $460 more a year if he secured only a standard rating.

So what determines your rating? Mostly your health and family history. To get the highest rating, insurers want to see that you're not overweight, have healthy blood pressure and have no family history of heart disease or cancer before age sixty.

Here's a list of some of the less commonly known risks that could lead to a hefty life insurance bill.

Mental health. Insurance companies are very interested in your mental health. While they won't ask you to submit to a mental checkup, they will inquire if you're taking an antidepressant and why.

Driving record. Aggressive drivers will be penalized; if you've had three or more moving violations in three years, you're going to pay more for your life insurance.

Credit history. Believe it or not, an insurer cares about your credit history. The thinking is that someone with a bad credit score may not pay his insurance premium. The other concern is that someone under financial stress may be more likely to take his own life.

Hobbies. Insurance companies find how you spend your free time quite compelling. While a typical person might think that someone who enjoys mountain climbing or skiing is healthy, an actuary sees these people as risks. In fact, they have a list of "risky" hobbies. If you engage in anything that's considered an extreme sport, including helicopter skiing or piloting a small plane, be prepared to write a larger check.

Travel. If your idea of a fun family trip is to take the kids trekking in Nepal, don't expect that preferred plus rating. For insurance purposes, you're considered a much higher risk than the parent who takes his children to Disney or the Bahamas. If you want to know which risky locales an underwriter may penalize you for, check out the U.S. State Department's travel warnings list.

out some quotes. While these prices are just estimates, they tend to be fairly accurate for healthy folks in their twenties and thirties, says AccuQuote's Udell. Either way, you'll eventually need to speak with an agent on the phone, who will further custom-tailor your quote and set up a physical exam.

You may wonder why you should even bother going online if you eventually need to speak with a real person. But the benefit of these Web sites is that they know you're shopping around and tend to offer very competitive prices. Some people also feel the entire sales experience is less pushy than sitting face-to-face with an insurance agent.

Either way, you'll have to take a physical and answer some personal health questions about yourself and your family. From this information, an underwriter will be able to determine your risk and put you into what's called a rating class. The higher your rating class, the less you'll pay in premiums.

How underwriters rate your risk of death will vary from one carrier to another, so go with an agent who represents different insurance companies—that way you can shop around for the cheapest policy.

As I mentioned earlier, life insurance policies—especially if you're going with term life—are a commodity product; it doesn't matter which company you go with, as long as it's highly rated. Insurance consultant Scott Simmonds says he recommends his clients go with an underwriter that's rated A or better by Weiss Ratings; you can feel confident that such a company will be around for the next thirty years.

INSURANCE TRUSTS

If you're buying a life insurance policy with proceeds that could trigger the federal estate tax, you may want to consider buying it through a life insurance trust. While no one knows what will happen with estate taxes after 2010, for 2009, all estates worth more than $3.5 million will have to pay it. That means your heirs would lose 45 percent of the money you leave them. (If the current law doesn't change, in 2011 all estates worth more than $1 million will get hit with a 55 percent estate tax.)

Keep in mind that if one spouse dies and the money goes to the other spouse, proceeds from an insurance policy are tax-free. (Different rules will apply to spouses who are not U.S. citizens.) It's once that money gets passed onto the children that it's subject to taxes. That means that if both parents pass away at the same time (or if the surviving spouse dies before spending the money) and the life insurance becomes part of the estate, the proceeds will get hit with the estate tax, leaving your children with roughly half of what you thought they needed to survive.

You can avoid this situation by placing the insurance in an irrevocable life insurance trust, so that money never gets taxed by Uncle Sam. The only downside is that you no longer own

LIFE INSURANCE LINGO

As if buying life insurance wasn't intimidating enough, the industry has its own language that may confuse you. Here is a quick reference for some of the most common terms you may come across.

Term life insurance. My favorite policy for young families. It covers policy-holders for a set period of time, say, ten, twenty or thirty years. Should you pass away during the life of your policy, your heirs receive the value of the policy. Term life premiums are considerably cheaper than whole life premiums.

Whole life insurance. Whole life combines term life with an investment component. So in addition to providing your heirs with insurance coverage, the insurance company is also investing money on your behalf. Over time, your policy will build up what's called a cash value (or surrender value), which is the amount of money you'd get if you tapped into the investment component of your insurance policy.

Universal life. Universal life is similar to whole life in that it offers a savings component. The main difference is that it allows you some flexibility with your premium payments. If money's tight, theoretically, you could pay a little less in the early years and make up for it later on. The danger is that if you pay too little during the first few years, your premiums could later skyrocket and become unaffordable.

Variable life. Variable life also looks and feels a lot like whole life. However, it lets you choose how you would like to invest the savings component of the policy from a handful of portfolios.

Return of premium. A hybrid between term life and whole life. You buy a policy for a set amount of time, and in the event you pass away, your heirs are paid the face value of your death benefit. Should you outlive your policy, the insurer sends you a tax-free check for the full amount that you've spent on premiums. It typically costs 50 percent more than a standard term policy.

Beneficiary. The person you name to receive the proceeds of your insurance policy. You can name both primary and secondary (in case your first choice is no longer living) beneficiaries, and they should always be people; the last thing you want to do is name your estate, since the proceeds could get tied up in the probate process.

Illustration. A proposal an insurance agent shows you, detailing an insurance policy's future payments, cash value and death benefits.

Rating classes. Insurance policies are priced based on your risk level, or what the industry calls your rating class. Traditionally, companies have used three classes—standard (highest rates), preferred (lower rates) and preferred plus (the best rates). Don't be surprised if you find insurers using more ratings in between those classes these days.

Death benefit. A lump sum payment the beneficiary of your life insurance policy receives upon your death.

the policy, the trust does. Translation: you can't change the beneficiaries, even if you get divorced. And you'll need to ask someone else or a bank to act as trustee. An estate-planning attorney can help you decide whether a life insurance trust makes sense for you, once you take all of your other assets into account.

If you already have a life insurance policy, you can place it in a trust, too. Just be aware that there is a three-year waiting period before it becomes active. If you should pass away before the three years, the money could still be subject to the estate tax.

In the next and final chapter, I'll discuss one other type of insurance families should consider buying to secure their family's future.

CHAPTER 12

ACCIDENTS HAPPEN... ARE YOU PREPARED?

Common Misconception:

My employer said it would take care of me if I ever get injured.

The Reality:

Your boss promised you the corner office, too, right? Your employers' disability insurance replaces up to only 60 percent of your salary, and those meager benefits expire after an average of five years.

The Bottom Line:

Consider buying a supplemental disability policy that will replace up to 80 percent of your lost income until you hit retirement age.

What's the final piece of any family's contingency plan? Disability insurance. Sound like a frivolous expense? Not for young parents who are just starting to accumulate assets and can't afford to take unpaid time off from the workforce.

Consider this: three out of ten workers will eventually become disabled before retirement, according to the Social

DISABILITY INSURANCE VERSUS WORKERS' COMPENSATION

Be careful not to confuse disability insurance with workers' comp. Disability insurance replaces your income if you can't work. Workers' comp pays your medical bills if you're injured on the job. If you do have an accident while you're working and become disabled, you could be eligible for both benefits.

Security Administration. And while you might think disabilities are typically caused by freak accidents, the majority of long-term absences from the workforce are actually due to illnesses, including cancer, heart disease and depression.

Disability insurance can be a real financial lifesaver and is truly essential for anyone who has dependents, as it replaces a portion of your income should you become disabled and no longer able to work. A typical group plan offered by an employer will replace up to 60 percent of your salary, although supplemental plans and individual policies that you buy on your own will often cover up to 70 percent or 80 percent. Benefits can last for a set number of years (typically two to five) or until you reach retirement age. If you pay the premium out of pocket—meaning your employer doesn't cover the tab—benefits are tax free.

While many midsized to large companies do provide short-term disability, far fewer offer long-term coverage. And if you work for a very small company, chances are you have no coverage at all. Indeed, 70 percent of the private sector workforce has no long-term disability insurance, according to the Social Security Administration. Translation: if you're assuming your employer will take care of you if you suffer a disability, you're probably wrong.

As I mentioned earlier, even if you are lucky enough to get disability insurance from an employer, it will typically replace just 60 percent of your income, cover you for no more than five years and be riddled with loopholes.

If you buy disability insurance on your own, which is called a supplemental plan, you can replace up to 80 percent of your income. (Unfortunately, you're not allowed to replace all of your income for fear that you may never try to go back to work.) You can also buy a plan that's far more comprehensive and covers you until you retire.

Odds are you're probably in a situation similar to Nancy Sherman's. Although Nancy and her husband knew disability was important—there's a greater chance a person will become disabled than pass away during his working years—they figured Nancy must have a pretty good policy through her employer since she works in the insurance industry. However, once Nancy was pregnant with her third child, she started reading through the fine print on her company's plan and realized her growing family needed more comprehensive coverage. She wanted to insure more of her income and to make sure that she would be paid if she couldn't perform her current job skills, as opposed to any occupation. So the Shermans bought supplemental disability insurance and rest easier knowing they can provide for their children should Nancy no longer be able to work.

This chapter will help you understand what type of coverage you have through your employer and how to figure out if it's adequate. If you decide you need more coverage, which most people do, I'll then walk you through what type of plan to buy. As with life insurance, buying a disability policy can be confusing. But after you read through this chapter you'll know exactly what to look for.

DISABILITY 101

There are two types of disability insurance. The first and most common is short-term disability, which is also known as sick leave. This kicks in as soon as you're unable to work due to an illness or childbirth. (If you recall, women can receive six to eight weeks of short-term disability after giving birth.)

The good news is that most midsized to large employers provide some type of short-term coverage, but the length can

THREE STEPS TO EVALUATING YOUR DISABILITY NEEDS

Here are three steps to help you figure out if you need disability insurance and, if you do, what type of policy to purchase.

Step 1:
Figure Out What You Already Have

If you have a corporate job, there's a decent chance you have some type of disability insurance. The trick is to figure out how comprehensive it is.

Step 2:
Determine Your Needs

Based on what you already have, determine if you need to purchase additional disability insurance. If you work for yourself, you'll definitely want to consider a policy, since you have no safety net.

Step 3:
Buying the Right Policy

Buying the right type of policy can be a bit complicated, so I'll clarify what to look for and what riders are worth the extra money. You don't, for example, need coverage from the first day of injury. You can save hundreds of dollars by waiting to receive benefits for ninety days. The Disability Insurance Comparison Shopping Chart in the Appendix can help you weigh your options.

꧁꧂

depend on how long you've worked for a certain company. Right now, only a handful of states (plus Puerto Rico) require employers to provide short-term disability insurance. (Hawaii, New Jersey, New York and Rhode Island require employers to provide at least twenty-six weeks of coverage. In California, employers are obligated to offer fifty-two weeks.)

SOCIAL SECURITY BENEFITS

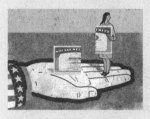 If you're severely disabled, Uncle Sam may help you out. Social Security provides long-term disability benefits to those who have been disabled for more than five months and whose disability is expected to either last a full year or end in death. You also must not be able to work at any occupation. While these benefits are nice to get if you qualify, they aren't very generous. According to a 2007 fact sheet from the Social Security Administration, the average monthly disability benefit is less than $1,000. Your check is based on your salary and the number of years you've worked and contributed to the Social Security system. And like with retirement, few people plan to retire on their Social Security checks alone. Check out the Social Security Administration's Web site (ssa.gov) for more information on applying for benefits.

The second type of coverage is long-term disability. It kicks in once your short-term benefits run out. While there are no state laws requiring employers to provide it, many do; it's estimated that about half of all midsized to large firms offer some form of long-term disability coverage.

Within the long-term disability category, there are group plans and individual policies. If you get long-term disability through your employer, that's considered a group plan. If you decide your plan through work doesn't provide you with enough coverage, you would buy a supplemental plan, which is considered an individual policy. You may also have the option to purchase more individual disability through your firm at a group rate, which is typically lower than if you buy it on your own. Or if you're self-employed or don't have any long-term disability through work, you can buy a regular individual plan.

MAKE AN APPOINTMENT
WITH HUMAN RESOURCES

Now that you understand the basics of disability insurance, it's time to figure out what you already have. For most of us, the only way to do that is to contact human resources. Ask for a complete breakdown of your coverage. It's not enough to be told you have short-term disability; you need to know how long it lasts and when it expires. You then need to know if there is a long-term disability plan, how much of your salary it replaces and what provisions it may include.

While most group long-term disability plans cover up to 60 percent of your income, the actual amount could be far less than that, since most plans have a monthly benefit cap of about $5,000, according to MetLife. (Some very generous employers may cap benefits at $10,000 a month.) You should also note that the 60 percent is only calculated against your salary, so if you receive the bulk of your compensation through bonuses, you're out of luck.

THE SELF-EMPLOYED NEED ADDED INCOME PROTECTION

If you're self-employed, it's especially important that you consider disability insurance. Remember, you aren't supplementing existing insurance, you're buying all of your coverage. A self-employed thirty-five-year-old male making $100,000 might pay around $1,500 a year (for a policy with a ninety-day waiting period) versus $570 for that same individual who was supplementing a group policy through work, according to Bryan Place, a certified financial planner and disability income specialist based in Manlius, New York.

Another problem: most group policies will pay benefits for only two years if you can't perform your job due to a disability. After that, you'll need to prove that you can't hold down *any* job to receive benefits.

YOUR NEEDS

Now that you know how much coverage you have, you should figure out if it's enough to raise your family on. Start off with the main breadwinner: What would happen if the family lost that income? Would it be a devastating loss? Or would the other spouse provide enough income for the family to thrive? If you're fairly wealthy and can live off savings, you don't necessarily need to replace all of your income. But if it would be a struggle to put food on the table and accomplish your various goals, including saving for retirement, you should consider a supplemental plan. You can go back to the Appendix and use the Monthly Budgeting Worksheet on page 186 to see where your family's budget would stand without one salary.

If one spouse isn't currently working, clearly the loss of the other spouse's income would be devastating. While you could make the argument that the nonworking spouse could find a job in this situation, it isn't always easy to immediately reenter the workforce. And there's a good chance his or her initial salary would be lower than before leaving the workforce to stay at home.

BUYING A POLICY

Unfortunately, you may have to pay up for your disability insurance. A thirty-five-year-old male, nonsmoking business executive would pay more than $1,000 in annual premiums for $3,500 per month in benefits delivered up to age sixty-five with a ninety-day waiting period according to Bryan Place.

As with life insurance, prices for a disability policy will vary based on your age, gender, amount of coverage and health status. But with disability, your occupation can also trigger a higher premium. Doctors and lawyers, for example, tend to pay much more since their skills are more specific to their jobs than a more versatile general business manager.

PICKING THE RIGHT POLICY

Unfortunately, buying disability insurance is quite confusing. Policies vary so much that if you try to skimp or neglect to read the fine print, you could ultimately end up with a worthless plan. You can keep track of what each policy you're considering has to offer with the Disability Insurance Comparison Shopping Chart in the Appendix. Here's what you should look for in a policy:

A longer waiting period. If you want to save considerable money on disability insurance, consider a policy with a longer waiting period. While some plans will kick in as soon as thirty or sixty days, you can save up to 40 percent on your premium if you wait six to twelve months. (You'll want to make sure you have an emergency fund to help cover your expenses until your insurance kicks in.) There's also no reason to pay more for a policy with only a thirty- or sixty-day waiting period if you're already covered by your employer's short-term disability insurance.

Your own occupation. You want a policy that will reimburse you if you can't perform your regular job skills, not if you can't physically work at all. So if you're a doctor, you want to be reimbursed if you can't treat patients, not if you can't flip a burger at McDonald's. While prices will vary, some carriers charge up to 40 percent more for this provision. Still, if you choose to go back to work in a new capacity, at least you know it's your choice, not an insurance company's.

Noncancelable. Provided you pay your premiums, the insurer can't cancel your policy. An insurer typically won't charge you extra for it, but you may still need to ask for this provision.

Guaranteed renewable. The insurer must renew your policy at the same price as long as you've been a good customer.

Again, a company may not increase your premium for this feature, but you may need to request it.

Coverage until age 65. If you want to protect your income until you retire, you'll want a policy with this rider. Just be aware that it could add another 15 percent to your premium.

———

If you can afford them, consider these further options:

Cost-of-living adjustment. This rider provides you with a cost-of-living adjustment so your benefits keep up with inflation. Carriers charge an extra 5 percent to 10 percent for it.

Residual disability. Residual disability comes into play when you can go back to work but your disability prevents you from making as much. It promises to make up the shortfall between what you earned before you got disabled and after. This could also be called a loss-of-earnings rider. Expect to pay 15 percent more for it.

Future purchase option. This one allows you to increase the amount of coverage as your income rises without undergoing another physical. Since no one knows when his or her health may start to deteriorate, it's a useful rider. Some insurers will include this option as part of their standard policy. If not, expect to pay up to an extra 10 percent for it.

MONEY-SAVING TIPS FOR EVERY STAGE

PREGNANCY AND BABY'S FIRST YEAR

1. REGISTER

Amount you'll save: hundreds of dollars
Don't be shy. Friends and family want to buy your baby gifts. Make it easy for them and register for all those items you need. You'll save the most if you include some big-ticket items—think stroller and high chair—and forfeit the burp cloths and pacifier covers.

2. BORROW BABY GEAR

Amount you'll save: anywhere from $40 to several hundred dollars
There's no need to buy a bouncy seat you'll use for only a few months when your friend has an old one sitting in her basement. Many parents are thrilled to lend out their infant gear, especially if they have a small child and won't need the stuff again until they have their second or third kid. It's a win/win for everyone.

3. Buy Used Stuff

Amount you'll save: 50 percent or more
There are only two items that product safety experts believe parents should always buy new: a crib and a car seat. That's because safety standards have changed over the years. For everything else, there's no reason you shouldn't go out and scour Craigslist or eBay for used high chairs and strollers. People often list their gently used stuff for 50 percent less than retail.

4. Snag Some Formula

Amount you'll save: at least $50
Hospitals and pediatricians' offices are overflowing with formula samples. Take as much as they're willing to give you. Most of the samples come in individual serving sizes, so they are especially useful for travel or when Grandma's babysitting. Breastfeeding moms who occasionally supplement with formula should especially be on the lookout for handouts. Otherwise, they risk wasting money opening large canisters of powdered formula they may not use before it spoils.

5. Avoid Unnecessary Items

Amount you'll save: $20 or more for each item
New parents are a marketer's dream. They convince moms and dads that an ear thermometer is a worthy investment (even though pediatricians argue they aren't accurate) and that baby wipes need to be warmed (even though the warmer itself poses a fire risk). Other hazardous items to avoid include bathtub seats (considered a drowning hazard), baby walkers (a child could roll down a set of steps) and crib bedding (baby could suffocate in blanket or a pillow). Check out NestingMode.com or ask a friend for a list of the bare necessities and stick with that.

6. Clip Coupons

Amount you'll save: $60 or more (if you're vigilant)
Always be on the lookout for coupons in the Sunday circular. You can also sign up at various baby product Web sites and get

BREAST-FEEDING

If your infant is exclusively formula-fed, expect to spend at least $1,500 during his or her first year. If you breast-feed, instead, the argument goes that the child eats for free. Well, that's not exactly true.

Most new mothers find there are all sorts of hidden start-up costs with breast-feeding. First, you'll probably want a breast milk pump ($270 for a double pump), a few nursing bras ($25–$45 each), nursing pads ($25) and lanolin cream ($10), and you may even want to invest in a nursing shirt or two ($35–$70). And don't forget, you'll need a system to freeze your milk and bottles for when you defrost it. You'll still come out way ahead of formula, but the savings may not be as great as you'd hoped if you only breast-feed for five or six months.

discounts mailed right to your front door or e-mailed to your in-box. Huggies, Enfamil and many of the other diaper and formula companies have Web sites that are just itching to advertise to you. Enfamil offers about $60 in formula checks during a baby's first year and Huggies mails a few dollars' worth of coupons every few months.

7. Select Generic Products

Amount you'll save: 25 percent
First-time moms are quick to wrap their baby's bum in Pampers and wash their clothes in Dreft. Veteran mothers don't bother since they know there's little difference from one brand to another. You can save up to 25 percent by buying generic or store brand products for everything from laundry detergent to baby wipes.

8. Buy in Bulk

Amount you'll save: at least 10 percent
New parents go through hundreds of diapers and wipes during an infant's first year. The easiest way to save money is to buy

these items in bulk from either a warehouse club store such as Costco or online at Amazon.com. While a typical drugstore may charge around 40 cents a diaper for Pampers, you can get them at Amazon (when you buy a value pack) for 22 cents.

9. BABYSITTING SWAP

Amount you'll save: $10 an hour
Looking for a night out with your spouse but don't want to spend on a babysitter? Consider watching your friend's child one night and then your friend can return the favor on an evening when you want to go out and catch the latest movie.

10. PLAYDATES RULE

Amount you'll save: up to $40 a session
Go out and make friends. Not only will you be less lonely during those first few months of parenthood, you'll also save a bundle. If you need to get out of the house and see other people, organize a weekly playdate (free!) instead of expensive Mommy and Me classes, which can cost as much as $20 to $40 a session.

TODDLER YEARS

1. DELAY PRESCHOOL

Amount you'll save: several thousand dollars
There's no reason a two-year-old needs a formal education. Wait until your little one is three or four and you can save thousands of dollars on preschool tuition.

2. ROTATE TOYS

Amount you'll save: $10 or more for each new toy you don't have to buy
Your children don't need more toys; they just need a break from their current plastic friends. Rather than keeping all the toys out, try keeping the bulk of them in a closet and bring out

only a few items at a time. That way, your little one will always be playing with toys that seem new to him.

3. MAKE YOUR OWN TOYS

Amount you'll save: $10 or more for each new toy you don't have to buy
When rotating the toys doesn't work, try creating an arts and crafts project at home. My friend's daughter likes to make necklaces out of dry pasta tubes and yarn. Can't think of anything on your own? Scour the Web for free ideas.

4. SHOP THE SALES

Amount you'll save: 20 percent to 50 percent
Veteran parents know that if they buy next year's wardrobe at the end-of-season sale they can save up to 50 percent. When children are small you rarely have to worry about things going out of style. Just shop the clearance sales and buy everything you need in the next year's size.

5. FIND FREE EVENTS

Amount you'll save: $20 or more per week
Get out the paper and search online for free children's events. Many libraries and bookstores offer free readings. Parks host concerts. Orchestras often have open rehearsals. Community centers often host free holiday events. And some museums charge only a suggested entrance fee, allowing you and your little ones to wander around for nothing. And don't forget to visit your local police or fire station.

6. POTTY-TRAIN EARLY

Amount you'll save: nearly $20 a week
I would never suggest forcing your child to potty-train before he's ready, but once you start to see those telltale signs, hop on it. The sooner he's using the toilet, the faster you'll stop wasting money on diapers.

THE DIAPER DEBATE

 Forget designer cribs and European high chairs. Those costs are minor compared with how much you could spend diapering your baby. According to *Consumer Reports,* disposable diapers can set parents back $1,500 to $2,000 before a child is potty trained.

If you're looking for ways to save money, you could consider buying two dozen cloth diapers for $20 and washing them yourself for next to nothing. But if you farm out the laundry to a diaper service, you don't really save much since it will cost you about $17 a week, according to the National Association of Diaper Services. That's roughly the same amount you'll spend on newborn disposable diapers.

Still, some parents argue that cloth diapers are cheaper over time since they lead to earlier potty training. Ann Krauss, a mother of four from Oro Valley, Arizona, used both cloth and disposable diapers. Her one child whom she saddled in cotton was wearing underpants nearly a year before the others. She believes the reason is because babies can feel the dampness in a cloth diaper, unlike a disposable diaper that keeps children dry.

7. AVOID FOODS THAT ARE MARKETED FOR TODDLERS

Amount you'll save: up to 50 percent

Once a child has teeth, she can pretty much eat anything you can. So there's no need to spend extra money on toddler foods, including yogurt and juice, in cute packaging. While the boxes may appeal to your little one, they cost more than the adult version and may contain more sugar. Formula companies also try to convince parents that they're better off giving their little ones "toddler formula" rather than milk. Not true. Once your infant is a year old, the American Academy of Pediatrics recommends whole milk, which can be 50 percent cheaper than formula per ounce.

ORGANIC VERSUS NONORGANIC FOODS

Many parents want to feed their children organic foods to protect them from harmful hormones, antibiotics, pesticides and other toxins. But all that protection gets expensive, costing as much as 50 percent more than conventional food. Here are some guidelines on what foods are worth paying up for and which ones may offer little more than empty promises.

Worth It

Meat and dairy. If you only have a limited budget for organics, spend that money on products that come directly from an animal, including milk, eggs, poultry and meat, according to *Consumer Reports*. These are the food items that are most likely to have potentially harmful hormones and antibiotics.

Produce. Next, buy the organic version of traditional fruits and vegetables that retain high levels of pesticide residue. While there are some exceptions, you're probably pretty safe if you stick with the "if you don't typically peel it, go organic" rule. The Environmental Working Group (EWG) recommends spending the extra money to buy the following produce organic:

Fruit	Vegetables
Apples	Bell peppers
Cherries	Celery
Imported grapes	Lettuce
Nectarines	Potatoes
Peaches	Spinach
Pears	
Red raspberries	
Strawberries	

Baby food. The organic jars of baby food are expensive but worth it if you're worried about pesticides. *Consumer Reports* argues that these foods are made up of condensed fruits or vegetables, a process that potentially concentrates pesticide residues.

Not Worth It

Seafood. Since there are no official USDA guidelines for seafood, there's no reason to seek out organic items. Instead, focus on whether a certain fish contains mercury, including tuna and swordfish, or high PCBs, which are found in bluefish.

Packaged foods. You can skip the packaged foods, too. *Consumer Reports* says that the more a food is processed, the less difference there is between the organic and traditional versions.

Labels

Finally, the only way to guarantee you're getting what you're paying for is if it's stamped "100% Organic" or has the official USDA Organic label. Other labels and claims, including "organic," could mean that as much as 30 percent of the ingredients aren't organic.

8. ACCEPT HAND-ME-DOWNS

Amount you'll save: $10–$15 per article of clothing
Don't be proud. If a friend offers you her older child's hand-me-downs, take them. Sure, the pants and shirts have been worn before, but they will feel new to you and your toddler. And let's face it, it's not like the new stuff you buy will stay new-looking for very long. Why not save the money?

9. FREQUENT CONSIGNMENT SHOPS

Amount you'll save: 50 percent or more
Remember how quickly infants grow tired of their toys? Toddlers are nearly as bad. So don't waste money buying a brand new tricycle or kitchen set when you can go to a consignment shop and pick one up for a fraction of the original cost. Give the wheels a good scrub and they'll look as good as new.

10. Kids-Eat-Free Night

Amount you'll save: $10 or more a meal

Parents can't cook every night. But a trip to a restaurant can get pretty expensive—and frustrating—when you're buying an entrée for a toddler who may not eat. (She said she wanted french fries!) The solution: look for a local eatery that offers a "kids-eat-free" night. The most common establishments that offer these deals are national chains such as Lone Star Steakhouse and Applebee's.

ELEMENTARY SCHOOL YEARS

1. Don't Overschedule Your Child

Amount you'll save: $200 or more a season

Let your kid just "be" some days and you'll not only foster independence and the ability to entertain himself, you can also save on that extra soccer league. If you want your child to get involved in some type of after-school activity, see if there's anything offered through the school itself or through a church or other community organizations. For example, membership in the Boy Scouts and Brownie Girl Scouts requires only a nominal fee.

2. Sibling Discounts

Amount you'll save: $10–$15 a session

If you have more than one child, try to coordinate their activities. Many facilities offer sibling discounts than can really add up over a few years. You'll also save yourself the hassle of coordinating class schedules since they will both be in the same location.

3. Buy the Smallest School Picture Package

Amount you'll save: $20 per photo session

School photos are expensive. While it's nice to have a few traditional pictures to put in the memory book, there's no reason to go all out and buy the largest package. Instead, buy the smallest package and send friends and family cute digital pictures of the family.

4. GET A FAMILY PLAN

Amount you'll save: $30 or more per month
Some parents believe their kids need a cell phone for safety reasons. If you're going to spring for one, get a family plan and share your minutes. For example, at Verizon and T-Mobile you pay one slightly cheaper price for two people to share minutes on one phone plan. But if you want to add a third phone for your child, then you'll start to see real savings, since it will only cost you $10.

5. SEMIPRIVATE LESSONS

Amount you'll save: up to 50 percent
It's great to encourage your kids to play tennis or pick up the violin. But there's no reason they need pricey private lessons. Share the hour with a friend and save up to 50 percent. As an added bonus, your child will now have someone to practice with between sessions.

6. PACK LUNCH

Amount you'll save: 25 percent or more
There's no reason your nine-year-old needs a catered lunch. It's not only cheaper for you to pack lunch, it's probably healthier, too.

7. BRING SNACKS

Amount you'll save: $2 or more on every snack
You can avoid pricey stops at a convenience store or food carts by carrying snacks for the kids wherever you go. Not only is it cheaper and more convenient, you'll also avoid moody behavior caused by low blood sugar.

VACATIONING WITH CHILDREN

Traveling with kids is many things, but cheap is not one of them. Once your child turns two, the Federal Aviation Administration requires you to buy a separate plane ticket for her. And unless you're comfortable tiptoeing around in the dark after your toddler's bedtime, you're going to want a suite or connecting hotel rooms. If you go to a resort, many charge extra for cribs or for meals your children will never eat.

Here are some ideas to help you keep the costs down so you can have your kids and travel, too.

Rent an Apartment

AMOUNT YOU'LL SAVE: UP TO 50 PERCENT

Forget staying in hotels. Families with small children can save money renting an apartment or house. You'll spend half as much for twice the space, says travel expert Pauline Frommer. Even better, you'll get a kitchen, so you'll always have fresh milk and snacks on hand. And at night you can put the little ones to bed, shut the bedroom door and enjoy the rest of your evening. Check out Web sites such as vrbo.com, HomeAway.com and Craigslist.com for vacation rentals.

Swap Your Home

AMOUNT YOU'LL SAVE: IT'S FREE

If you're lucky enough to live someplace other people like to visit, you could swap your home with another family and vacation for next to nothing. Advertise your house as "family-friendly" (mention if you have a crib or toddler bed) and you may get offers to trade for a house with similar accommodations. That means you don't need to schlep your portable crib along. You can find a swapping partner at HomeExchange.com or HomeLink.org.

Go Off-Season

AMOUNT YOU'LL SAVE: 15 PERCENT TO 50 PERCENT

Once your kids hit elementary school, you're stuck traveling during their vacations, paying peak prices or pulling them out of school. So if your kids are under five, now's the time to travel during the off-season and take advantage of discounted rates on everything from airfares to hotel rooms, resorts and cruises.

Take a Road Trip

AMOUNT YOU'LL SAVE:
HUNDREDS OF DOLLARS FOR PLANE TICKETS

Yes, you will hear the dreaded phrase "Are we there yet?" more than you would like, but the time-tested road trip can be a great way to save money and see the United States. If theme parks aren't your style, consider taking the kids to a U.S. national park. There are nearly four hundred of them across the country, offering everything from boating and camping to digging for dinosaur fossils. And many of the parks, including Yellowstone National Park and Yosemite National Park, offer Junior Ranger programs that can enhance your trip through planned activities.

Pack Light

AMOUNT YOU'LL SAVE: $20 TO $50 PER BAG IN FEES

Avoid the temptation to bring all of the kids' toys with you when traveling. First, it's tough to maneuver multiple suitcases, strollers, car seats and kids through a crowded airport. And now airlines are restricting how much luggage you can bring with you. If your bags cross over into the "heavy" category, you'll have to pay a $50 fee. Remember, if you rent a house, you can usually do laundry once you arrive, allowing you to bring less stuff.

8. IMPLEMENT AN ALLOWANCE

Amount you'll save: as much as you budget for

It's important to teach kids the value of money from an early age. One way to do that is with an allowance. As soon as you successfully get the program going, you'll save money. When your son has his own spending money, it will be up to him to decide what toys he wants and which ones aren't necessary. Without his own cash, you'll inevitably get strong-armed into spending more than you want on video games and other child-related paraphernalia.

9. Share a Hotel Room

Amount you'll save: $150 or more a night

If you share a hotel room (get a room with two double beds) while vacationing, you can save a bundle. Since babies typically go to sleep much earlier than adults, special accommodations are often useful. But once your children hit elementary school, they'll stay up later and you won't have to worry so much about tiptoeing around in the dark after the little ones are in bed.

APPENDIX

Subtract the family's expenses from take-home pay in both scenarios to determine which one provides the highest monthly cash flow.

	One Salary	Two Salaries
Monthly Take-Home Pay*	_____	_____
Monthly Expenses	_____	_____
Child care (day care, etc.)**	_____	_____
Other child-related costs***	_____	_____
Commuting costs	_____	_____
Cost of work clothing and dry cleaning	_____	_____
Meals at work	_____	_____
Unreimbursed employee costs (work-related tools, supplies, travel, entertainment, gifts, etc.)	_____	_____
Other costs (publications, memberships, etc.)	_____	_____
Total Expenses	_____	_____
Remaining Cash Flow (subtract total expenses from take-home pay)	_____	_____

* Use your after-tax income, then factor in health insurance premium deductions and flexible spending account contributions. Note: make sure to factor in if your tax bracket will change going from two incomes to one. (Check irs.gov for tax bracket information.)

** Enter any expenses beyond your flexible spending contribution.

*** Keep in mind, stay-at-home parents often like to sign up for Mommy and Me classes and other activities.

DISABILITY INSURANCE
COMPARISON SHOPPING CHART

Comparing multiple disability insurance policies can be confusing at best. Use this chart to keep track of the various benefits each company offers so you don't pick a plan that doesn't provide you with the coverage you need.

Feature	Company A	Company B	Company C	Company D
Insurance company name				
Agent name				
Agent licensed in your state?				
Does the agent sell other lines of insurance?				
Agent's experience selling long- term disability?				
Agent's time in insurance business?				
Insurance company A. M. Best rating				
Insurance company Weiss rating				
Dollar benefit amount				
Benefit period				
Elimination/ waiting period				

Feature	Company A	Company B	Company C	Company D
Cost-of-living adjustment				
Future increase in coverage provision				
Automatic increase in coverage				
Maximum benefit for mental or nervous conditions				
Maximum benefit for alcohol and drug claims				
Exclusion for claims resulting from a crime				
Exclusion for claims resulting from war				
Annual premium				
Rider premiums				

Source: Scott Simmonds

MONTHLY BUDGETING WORKSHEET

Monthly Expenses	Amount
Basic Necessities	
Mortgage/rent	_____
Credit card payment(s)	_____
Other debt payment(s)	_____
Utilities	_____
Health insurance	_____
Auto insurance	_____
Car payment	_____
Medications	_____
Commuting	_____
Telephone/cell phone	_____
Groceries	_____
Diapers	_____
Formula	_____
Child care/preschool	_____
Retirement savings (401(k), IRA, etc.)	_____
Other Expenses	
Internet service	_____
Cable	_____
Baby gear	_____
Child-related activities	_____
Babysitters	_____
Clothing	_____
Grooming (haircuts, etc.)	_____
Entertainment (movies, etc.)	_____
Eating out (including lunch at work)	_____
Dry cleaning	_____
Hobbies	_____
Total Expenses	$_____
Enter Monthly Income:*	$_____
Subtract Total Expenses:	$_____
Available Cash	$_____

*Use your after-tax income.

ACKNOWLEDGMENTS

This book was possible thanks to the support of my editors, family, friends and the many financial experts who shared their knowledge with me.

I am grateful to SmartMoney.com, where I worked for more than a decade, for its commitment to personal finance and for helping me develop the skills to cover this very important subject matter.

Special thanks to my former editors at SmartMoney.com, including Stephanie AuWerter and Ray Hennessey, and to Bill Shaw, SmartMoney's publisher, for all of their support.

A special thank you to Arnold Dolin for reading my proposal and giving me the confidence to pursue my book. To Bob Sabat who encouraged and helped me bring this idea to *The Wall Street Journal*. To Roe D'Angelo, the director of books and special projects at *The Wall Street Journal*, who believed in the book and gave me the opportunity to write it. To Lindsay Orman at the Crown Publishing Group for her tireless work editing the chapters and making the manuscript what it is today. And to all the very talented folks who designed, copyedited and vetted this book. Thank you all so much.

Thank you to the dozens of parents who took the time out of their busy lives to share their personal stories with me. Despite juggling multiple responsibilities, they all managed to call me back during nap times or after putting their kids to bed. I would especially like to thank Chetna Bansal, Mona and Michael Berman, Dave Bieler, Nancy Bisaha, Amy Fisher, Lia Gravier, Lisa Green, Ann Krauss, Samantha Lau, David Leibowitz, Ambre Proulx, Lucy Ritter, Gabrielle Rosenfeld, Alex Sasieta, Fiona Schaeffer, Dorothea Schlosser, Jennifer and Steven Share, Nancy Sherman, Beth Stalter, Tawnya Stone, Kristine Suzuki, Alan Wang, and Laurie and Greg Wetzel.

I want to express my gratitude to Marty Fass for reviewing my chapter on taxes and to Joanne Sternlieb for her legal expertise on wills and trusts.

I'm especially grateful to my parents, who supported my decision to enter journalism and put me through j-school. My mother-in-law, Susan, my biggest fan, who helped babysit while I wrote this book. And to my sister, Karen, and sister-in-law, Stef, who helped connect me to their friends with children.

Most of all, I want to thank my beloved husband, Rick, for his never-ending faith in what I can accomplish. And also for his countless hours reading over my manuscript and providing helpful suggestions, all while working at his own demanding job. And, of course, to my daughter, who provided the inspiration for this book.

INDEX

accidents, 161–69
action plan for parents, 3
adoption:
    and maternity leave, 14
    and taxes, 49–50, 54
alimony, 47
allowance, child's, 181
apartment rental, for vacations, 180
au pairs:
    costs, 78–79, 83
    difficulties with, 86
    hiring, 90
    interview questions for, 91
    pros and cons, 83, 85–86

baby, spending all your time with, 21–22
baby food, 176
baby formula, 171
baby items:
    avoiding unnecessary items, 171
    borrowing, 17, 27, 170
    bulk purchases, 172–73
    clipping coupons for, 171–72
    from consignment shops, 177
    diapers, 172–73, 174, 175
    generic, 172
    modest financial outlay for, 17
    registration for, 17, 170
    saving money on, 26–28, 170–73
    used, 171
babysitters,
    costs, 78, 82
    hiring, 88–90
    interview questions for, 89
    legal considerations, 82, 84–85

pros and cons, 81–83
Social Security for, 85
babysitting swap, 173
background checks, 88, 89
back to work, 29–32, 33–42
    decision to make, 17–18, 20–21, 24, 183
    and employee benefits, 35, 53–54
    financial considerations of, 34–36
    handling tough questions about, 31
    negotiating your terms, 35, 36–38
    pay cut, 36
    reentry plan, 22, 31–32
    staying connected to the workforce, 29–30
    for trial period, 37
    worksheet, 24, 183
    written proposal for, 37
beneficiary, defined, 159–60
breast-feeding, saving money in, 172
budgeting:
    for child's allowance, 181
    for college savings, 111, 186
    for maternity leave, 10–13, 14
    monthly worksheet, 186
    for second and subsequent children, 26
    for stay-at-home parents, 22, 24–26, 183
bulk purchases, 172–73

cars, two-car family, 68
car seats, 17, 171
cell phones, family plan for, 179

charitable donations, tax deduction for, 53
child care, 75–92
  au pairs, 78–79, 83, 85–86, 90, 91
  babysitters, 78, 81–83, 88–90
  backup, 41
  costs of, 34, 41, 76–80
  day care facilities, 79–80, 86–88, 90, 92
  employee benefit vs. tax credit, 53–54
  finding the right fit, 77, 80–81
  FSA for, 41, 80, 85
  hiring, 77, 88–92
  legal considerations, 84–85
  tax credit for, 50
children:
  allowances for, 181
  clothing sales, 174
  costs of, 1
  custodial parent of, 47
  custodian for property of, 135, 139
  disabled, 127
  elementary school years, 178–81
  food for, 175
  free events for, 174
  guardian for, 129–31, 138–39
  hand-me-down clothing for, 177
  kiddie tax, 50, 117
  kids-eat-free night, 178
  and letter of intent, 127
  overscheduling, 178
  potty-training, 174
  reading with, 182
  school pictures, 178–79
  semiprivate lessons, 179
  sharing custody of, 47
  sibling discounts, 178
  sick, 63, 80, 87
  Social Security numbers for, 45
  with special needs, 127
  tax credits for, 48
  tax returns for, 46
  toys, 173–74
  trust funds for, see trust funds
  vacations with, 180–81, 182
child support, 47
city life:
  advantages, 58–59
  disadvantages, 59–60
  expenses, 66–67
  savings, 67

clothing:
  consignment shops, 177
  hand-me-down, 177
  sales, 174
COBRA, 19, 98–99
coinsurance, 97
college:
  expected family contribution, 122
  federal work-study program, 120
  financial aid, 118–21, 122
  government loan programs, 121
  merit grants, 119
  Pell grants, 119
  Perkins loans, 120
  private loans, 121
  scholarships, 119, 120
  Stafford loans, 120
  state grants, 119
college savings, 27, 107–18
  basic 529 plan, 112–13, 122
  budgeting for, 111, 186
  changing rules for, 122
  Coverdell education savings account, 116–17, 122
  Crummey trust, 118
  529 prepaid tuition plan, 113
  independent 529 plan, 115–16
  as parental assets, 122
  planning now for, 109
  selecting a vehicle for, 109, 112–21
  setting goals for, 109
  state tuition plans, 113, 115
  and taxes, 51
  UGMA and UTMA, 117–18, 122
  Upromise.com, 113
commuting:
  costs of, 68, 69
  FSA covering costs of, 42
  and sick child, 63, 80
  telecommuting, 37–38
  time for, 63
consignment shops, 177
coupons, clipping, 171–72
Coverdell education savings account, 116–17, 122
credit card debt, lowering and/or eliminating, 16, 111
credit history, and insurance, 157

crib, buying new, 171
Crummey trust, 118
custodial accounts, vs. trusts, 139, 141, 142
custodial parent, 47
custodian, for children's property, 135, 139

day care facilities:
  arranging, 90
  changing, 90
  costs, 79–80
  interview questions for, 92
  preschool component in, 79
  pros and cons, 86–88
  spreading germs, 87
death benefit, 160
debt:
  consolidation of, 16
  elimination of, 111
dependent care, 38, 41, 45, 50
dependent exemption, 45, 46–48
diapers:
  bulk purchases of, 172–73
  cloth vs. disposable, 175
  generic, 172
  and potty-training, 174
disability, child with, 127
disability insurance, 161–69
  for breadwinner, 167
  buying the right policy, 164, 167–69
  caps on, 14
  comparison shopping chart, 184–85
  cost-of-living adjustment, 169
  from employer, 162, 166
  evaluating your needs, 164
  fine print on, 168
  future purchase option, 169
  group policies, 166
  guaranteed renewable, 168–69
  long-term, 165
  and maternity leave, 14
  noncancelable, 168
  residual disability, 169
  for self-employed persons, 166
  short-term, 14, 162, 163–65
  and Social Security, 165
  supplemental plan, 162–63
  waiting period for, 168
  workers' compensation vs., 162
  and your occupation, 168

discrimination:
  Pregnancy Discrimination Act, 13
  and your FMLA rights, 18, 19
divorce, and taxes, 47
doctors:
  and health insurance, 100
  primary care (PCPs), 96
donations, tax deduction for, 53
driving record, and insurance, 156
driving vacation trips, 181

earned income tax credit, 48–49
eating out:
  cutting back on, 16, 27
  kids-eat-free night, 178
education:
  college, see college; college savings
  Coverdell savings account, 116–17, 122
  financial assistance for, 110
  Lifetime Learning tax credit, 51–52, 116
  parochial schools, 110
  preschool, 110, 173
  public vs. private schools, 57, 60, 66, 110, 114–15
  scholarships, 119, 120
employer identification number, 84
Employment Eligibility Verification, 84
entertainment, cutting costs of, 16
EPO (exclusive provider organization) health plans, 99
Equal Employment Opportunity Commission (EEOC), 13
estate planning:
  assets that pass outside of a will, 135
  attorney for, 133
  see also trust funds; will
estate taxes, 134, 155, 158
executor:
  asking permission of, 132–33
  choosing, 131–32
  naming in the will, 134
exurban life, 62–65
  advantages, 63–64
  disadvantages, 64–65
  expenses, 69–70
  master-planned communities, 65, 70
  savings, 70–71

Fair Credit Reporting Act, 89
Family and Medical Leave Act
    (FMLA):
  adoption and foster benefits
    under, 14
  and demotion, 18
  and paternity leave, 12
  provisions of, 13
  your rights under, 19
family plans:
  for cell phones, 179
  sibling discounts, 178
fish, 177
529 basic college savings plan,
    112–13, 122
529 independent plan, 115–16
529 prepaid tuition plan, 113
flexible spending account (FSA):
  child care expenses, 41, 80, 85
  commuting costs, 42
  dependent care, 41
  health care expenses, 40, 54, 105
food:
  organic vs. nonorganic, 176–77
  packaged, 177
  school lunches, 179
  snacks, 179
  for toddlers, 175
formula samples, 171
foster parents, and maternity leave,
    14
free events, 174
furnishings, 70

garbage pickup, 68
generic products, 172
gift taxes, 115
GTM Payroll Services (GTM.com),
    84
guardians:
  asking permission of, 132–33
  choosing, 129–31
  court-appointed, 138–39
  multiple, 131
  naming in the will, 134
  sample letter to, 136–37

hand-me-down clothing, 177
happiness, 57–58
health, neglecting your own, 104–5
health care, preventive, 106
health care expenses:
  as employee benefit vs. tax credit,
    54

FSA, 40, 54, 105
  HSA for, 41, 105
  keeping receipts for, 103–4
  out-of-pocket, 105
  tax write-off for, 105–6
health insurance, 93–106
  adjustable, 38
  affordable, 34
  for children (SCHIP), 94
  and COBRA, 19, 98–99
  coinsurance, 97
  corporate plans, 39–40
  costs of, 94
  doctors covered by, 100
  employer self-funded plans, 95,
    103, 104
  EPO plans, 99
  fighting a claim, 102–3
  fine print in, 99–100
  generic medications, 101
  HMOs, 96–97
  individual policies, 98–99
  loss of, 19, 21
  medicines, 101, 103
  open enrollment, 104
  POS plans, 99
  PPOs, 97
  and preexisting conditions, 98
  premium cost of, 23
  prescriptions, 101
  pretax dollars for, 95, 105
  smart use of, 95
  state regulation of, 98, 102–3
  understanding your coverage, 95
health savings accounts (HSAs), 41,
    105
HMOs (health maintenance
    organizations), 96–97
hobbies and interests, and
    insurance, 157
home, see residence
home equity, and financial aid
    calculations, 121–22
Hope credit, 116
hotel room, sharing, 182
household bills:
  cutting back on, 16–17
  and suburban living, 68
house-swapping vacations, 180

independence, loss of, 25
independent 529 college savings
    plan, 115–16
insurance, 111

beneficiaries of, 135, 159–60
coinsurance, 97
and credit history, 157
disability, *see* disability insurance
fighting a claim, 102–3
health, *see* health insurance
home owner, 68–69
life, *see* life insurance
rating/risk classes, 160
reading the fine print of, 99–100
state regulation of, 98, 102–3
interviews:
  of au pairs, 91
  of day care facilities, 92
  informational (job), 30–31
  of nannies, 89
intestate, dying, 126
IRA, spousal, 28
IRS, 43–54
  and child care, 84–85
  and commuting costs, 42
  employer identification number, 84
  and spousal IRA, 28
  Web site, 28
  see also taxes

joint assets, 135
joint will, 133

kiddie tax, 50, 117
kids-eat-free night, 178

Labor Department, states, 13
Labor Department, U.S.:
  and FMLA rights, 19
  Web site, 19
lawn care, 68
leave:
  for adopting and foster parents, 14
  end of, 17–18
  see also maternity leave
lessons, semiprivate, 179
letter of intent, 127
life changes, and taxes, 44, 45–46
life insurance, 148–60
  beneficiaries of, 159–60
  beyond employer's plan, 150, 152
  for breadwinner, 153
  buying a policy, 151, 155, 157–58
  choosing the product, 154–55
  cost, 154, 156
  death benefit, 160

employer's plan, 152
and estate taxes, 158
evaluating the need for, 150, 151, 152
and family balance sheet, 152
goal of, 154
how much to buy, 153–54
and investment fees, 155
language of, 159–60
and pregnancy, 149
rating/risk classes, 156–58, 160
return-of-premium policy, 155, 159
selecting the policy, 151
for stay-at-home parent, 153
term life, 154–55, 156, 159
universal life, 159
variable life, 159
Web sites, 155
whole life, 154–55, 159
and your lifestyle, 153–54
life insurance trust, 151, 158, 160
lifestyle:
  and choice of home, 55, 57–58
  and life insurance coverage, 153–54
Lifetime Learning credit, 51–52, 116
long-term disability insurance, 165

maternity leave, 9–19
  budgeting for, 10–13, 14
  end of, 17–18
  estimating money needed for, 11
  money expected during, 14–15
  saving for, 11, 15–17
  and short-term disability insurance, 14
  steps to, 11
  vacation time for, 15
  what you're entitled to, 11
  see also leave
Medicaid, and disabled children, 127
medical expenses, tax deduction for, 51
medicines, 101, 103
mental health, and insurance, 156
mercury, in fish, 177
merit grants, 119
merit scholarships, 119, 120
Mommy and Me, 173
MyStateWill.com, 126

nannies, *see* babysitters
networking, 30

organic vs. nonorganic foods, 176–77
overscheduling your child, 178

parochial schools, 110
paternity leave, and FMLA, 12
PCBs, in fish, 177
PCPs (primary care physicians), 96
Pell grants, 119
Perkins loans, 120
phone bills, cutting back on, 16–17
playdates, 173
POS (point-of-service) health plans, 99
potty-training, 174
PPOs (preferred provider organizations), 97
pregnancy:
   and life insurance, 149
   money-saving tips, 170
Pregnancy Discrimination Act, 13
preschool:
   co-ops, 110
   delaying, 173
   financial assistance for, 110
   public vs. private, 110
prescriptions, 101
professional organizations, 30
professional skills, updating, 51–52

reading, 182
registration, for baby gifts, 17, 170
residence, 55–71
   city, 58–60, 66–67
   doing the math, 56, 65–71
   exurb, 62–65, 69–71
   financial commitments for, 17
   first-time home buyers, 52–53
   furnishing, 70
   and happiness, 57–58
   hidden considerations, 57, 70
   home owner's insurance, 68–69
   and lifestyle, 55, 57–58
   location preference, 56
   master-planned communities, 65, 70
   moving costs, 70
   moving to save money, 27–28, 65
   and schools, 57
   selling a home, 52
   suburban, 60–62, 67–69

residual disability, 169
restaurants:
   cutting back on, 16, 27
   kids-eat-free nights, 178
retirement savings, 111
   continuing contributions to, 26, 28, 39
   employer matching, 39
   exempt from financial aid calculations, 121
   spousal IRA, 28
   tax-advantaged, 34, 39
   value of, 24
return-of-premium life insurance policy, 155, 159

safe deposit box, 137
sales, shopping for, 174
saving:
   city life, 67
   for college, *see* college savings
   exurban life, 70–71
   health savings account, 41
   for maternity leave, 11, 15–17
   for retirement, *see* retirement savings
   spousal IRA, 28
   suburban life, 69
   tax, *see* taxes
saving tips, 16–17, 170–82
   allowances, 181
   baby gear, 26–28
   baby's first year, 170–73
   babysitting swap, 173
   breast-feeding, 172
   bulk purchases, 172–73
   cell phones, 179
   clipping coupons, 171–72
   consignment shops, 177
   diapers, 172–73, 174, 175
   elementary school years, 178–81
   family plans, 179
   food, 175–77, 179
   formula samples, 171
   free events, 174
   hand-me-downs, 177
   kids-eat-free night, 178
   overscheduling, 178
   playdates, 173
   potty-training, 174
   pregnancy, 170
   preschool, delay, 173
   reading, 182

registration, 17, 170
sales, 174
school lunches, 179
school pictures, 178–79
semiprivate lessons, 179
sibling discounts, 178
toddler years, 173–78
toys, 173–74, 177
vacations, 180–81, 182
school lunches, 179
school pictures, saving money on, 178–79
seafood, 177
second child, budgeting for, 26
self-employed persons, disability insurance for, 166
short-term disability insurance, 14, 162, 163–65
sibling discounts, 178
snacks, 179
Social Security, 21
for babysitters, 85
child's SS number, 45
and disability, 165
Web site, 45
special needs, child with, 127
spousal IRA, 28
Stafford loans, 120
State Children's Health Insurance Program (SCHIP), 94
State Department, U.S. travel warnings, 157
state employment office, 84
stay at home:
budgeting for, 22, 24–26, 186
decision to make, 17–18, 20–21, 24, 183
doing the math, 22, 23–24
emotional cost of, 25
life insurance for, 153
reentry plan, 22, 31–32
steps for, 22
worksheet, 24, 183
suburban life, 60–62
advantages, 61
disadvantages, 61–62
expenses, 67–69
savings, 69
Supplemental Security Income (SSI), 127

taxes, 43–54
and adoption, 49–50, 54
on alimony, 47
and charitable donations, 53
child and dependent care credit, 50
child's tax return, 46
child support, 47
child tax credit, 48
in city life, 66
college savings accounts, 51
dependent exemption, 45, 46–48
and divorce, 47
doing the math, 44
earned income tax credit, 48–49
employee benefits vs. tax credits or deductions, 53–54
estate, 134, 155, 158
for first-time home buyers, 52–53
gift, 115
health expenses, 105–6
kiddie, 50, 117
and life changes, 44, 45–46
Lifetime Learning credit, 51–52
medical expenses deduction, 51
options, 44
and retirement savings, 34, 39
and selling a home, 52
Social Security numbers, 45
and unforseen circumstances, 52
withholding, for nanny or babysitter, 84
telecommuting, 37–38
term life insurance, 154–55, 156, 159
TIAA-CREF Intuition Financing plan, 115–16
toddler years, saving tips for, 173–78
toys:
from consignment shops, 177
making your own, 174
rotating, 173–74
see also baby items
travel:
and life insurance, 157
State Department warnings, 157
vacations, 180–81, 182
trust funds, 138–47
attorney for, 139
boilerplate language in, 145
choosing a trustee for, 143–44
control in, 139, 142
Crummey, 118
custodial accounts vs., 139, 141, 142

trust funds (*cont.*)
decisions about, 140–41
drafting, 145, 147
legal contract for, 142
life insurance, 151, 158, 160
property guardian appointed for, 138–39
sample letter to trustee, 146–47
separate for each child, 145
steps for drafting, 142
trustee's job, 144

unemployment, 19
Uniform Gift to Minors Act (UGMA), 117–18, 122
Uniform Transfer to Minors Act (UTMA), 117–18, 122, 139
universal life insurance, 159
Upromise.com, 113
urban living:
advantages, 58–59
disadvantages, 59–60
expenses, 66–67
savings, 67

vacations:
apartment rental, 180
with children, 180–81, 182
driving trips, 181
house swapping, 180
maternity leave during, 15
off-season, 180
packing for, 181
sharing hotel room, 182
variable life insurance, 159

whole life insurance, 154–55, 159
will, 125–37
assets passing outside, 135
attorney for, 133
avoiding, 127–29
and custodial accounts, 139, 141, 142
and custodian, 135, 139
and disabled child, 127
drafting, 133–35
dying without (intestate), 126
and estate taxes, 134
executor for, 131–33, 134

and financial plan, 132
joint, 133
MyStateWill.com, 126
naming a guardian, 129–31, 132–33, 134
sample letter to guardian, 136–37
steps, 128
updating, 126, 128
where to keep, 137
work, 20–32
benefits of, 21, 23, 34, 35, 38–42
benefits vs. tax credits, 53–54
decision to stay or leave, 17–18, 20–21, 24, 183
demotion, 18
earning potential, 34
flexible hours, 37
and FMLA, 13, 19
foot in the door, 31–32
and FSA, 40, 41, 42, 54, 80, 85, 105
human resources department, 38
informational interviews, 30–31
networks at, 30
part-time, 21, 29, 31–32, 37, 38
productivity, 37
professional organizations, 30
returning to, *see* back to work
staying connected to, 29–30
staying in the workforce, 34–36
telecommuting, 37–38
trial period for, 37
two working spouses, 36
updating professional skills, 51–52
workers' compensation coverage:
disability insurance vs., 162
for household employees, 85
Working Mother, 37, 38
working papers, for nannies and babysitters, 88
worksheets:
Disability Insurance Comparison Shopping Chart, 184–85
Monthly Budgeting, 186
Working vs. Staying Home, 24, 183
work-study programs, 120

ABOUT THE AUTHOR

STACEY L. BRADFORD covers personal finance with a focus on family finance, health care, health insurance, life insurance, real estate, elder care and the job market as a feature writer and blogger. She was an associate editor at SmartMoney.com for more than ten years.

Stacey's articles have appeared in *The Wall Street Journal*'s Sunday Journal, on RealEstateJournal.com, CareerJournal.com, AOL, MoneyWatch.com, and Yahoo! Finance. She appears regularly on TV and radio—she's appeared on CNN Headline News, Fox News, Fox Business, CNBC, CBS, Wall Street Journal Radio Network and CBS Radio—on topics ranging from family finance and real estate to health insurance and retirement.

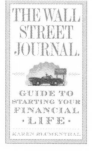

The Wall
SPECIAL OFFER

The One Investment You Can Count On.

2 WEEKS FREE!

YES! Send me **2 FREE WEEKS** of The Wall Street Journal and also enter my subscription for an additional 26 weeks at the money-saving rate of only $49.00 — just 32¢ a day! I receive 28 weeks in all and **SAVE 65%** off the regular rate.

Order now! ▶

Name _____

Address _____

City _____

State _____ Zip _____

2PCJM

CALL NOW FOR FASTER SERVICE!
1-800-620-5798

DOWJONES

THE WALL STREET JOURNAL.

The Guide in your hands is a great way to start building wealth.

The best way to keep your assets growing is to read THE WALL STREET JOURNAL!

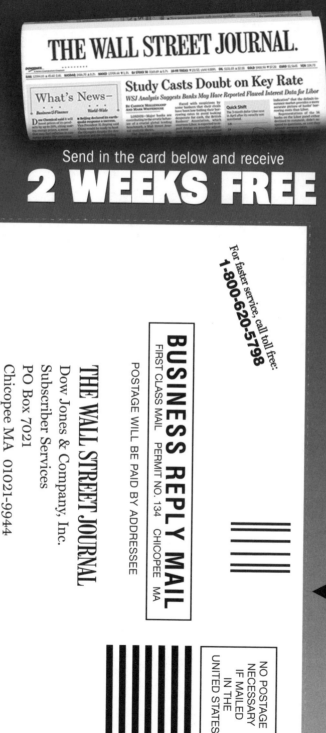

Send in the card below and receive

2 WEEKS FREE

For faster service, call toll free:
1-800-620-5798

POSTAGE WILL BE PAID BY ADDRESSEE

BUSINESS REPLY MAIL
FIRST CLASS MAIL   PERMIT NO. 134   CHICOPEE MA

THE WALL STREET JOURNAL
Dow Jones & Company, Inc.
Subscriber Services
PO Box 7021
Chicopee MA 01021-9944

NO POSTAGE
NECESSARY
IF MAILED
IN THE
UNITED STATES

Order now!